Praise for Jane Atkinson and *The Wealthy Speaker*...

"I wish I had *The Wealthy Speaker* as a roadmap when I got into this business 20 years ago ... I could have saved a ton of time and money!"

— Amanda Gore, CSP
Author of *You Can Be Happy*

"Before you open your mouth to speak be sure to open Jane Atkinson's book to learn how, to whom, about what, and how much you should get paid to speak."

— Larry Thompson, Hollywood Film Producer and Manager
Author of *SHINE: A Powerful 4-Step Formula for Being a Star at Anything You Do*

"Jane has written the definitive book on how to speak and get paid, as well as, how to fill your calendar with the right speaking engagements!"

— Mark LeBlanc
Author of *Growing Your Business!*

"What are you waiting for? *Run*, don't walk, to read this book! If you apply even one idea, you'll take a quantum leap forward in your career! There are gems for both beginner and experienced speakers alike."

— Andrea H. Gold
President, Gold Stars Speakers Bureau

"If you really want to know how to succeed as a professional speaker, this is the ultimate book to read. While many talk about what to do to succeed, Jane has actually done it. She knows what really works and shares her insights with you in *The Wealthy Speaker 2.0.*"

— Mark Sanborn, CSP, CPAE
Author, *The Fred Factor*

"Jane is one of the true pros in the speaker marketing business. Her knowledge and experience are invaluable for anyone who strives to be a wealthy speaker."

— Vic Osteen
General Manager, WIN Seminars

"*The Wealthy Speaker* is the bible of the speaking industry. Make a date with Jane Atkinson to make your business soar. It will be the best investment you have ever made."

— Betska K-Burr, MPC Vice President,
Coaching and Leadership International Inc.

"*The Wealthy Speaker* is an incredibly unique and valuable book for anyone wanting to get into this business or dramatically increase their existing success. Jane's style is engaging and highly entertaining while providing concrete, solid advice along with practical exercises. I highly recommend this book to my current and aspiring colleagues."

— Jim Clemmer, Speaker, Workshop Leader
Author, *The Leaders Digest*

"Speaking success is up to you. *The Wealthy Speaker* is certain to improve your odds."

— Brian Palmer, President
National Speakers Bureau, Chicago

"So you want to be a professional speaker? Buy this book and commit it to memory. It covers every aspect of speaking from the how tos to the how not toos! Jane Atkinson is simply the best teacher in the business. How do I know? We worked together for two years and my speaking business exploded. She's the best."

—Dr. Peter Legge, CSP, CPAE, HoF, LLD (hon)
Speaker/Author/Businessman

"I've read Jane's new book cover to cover and the entire time I found myself wishing I had a guide like this to use 20 years ago! As the management company for ten "Wealthy Speakers", I can guarantee that this book is a *must read* for anyone thinking about getting into the speaking business *and* for all of us that are already in the business including staff and bureau professionals! Jane's no-nonsense approach and easy to use coaching exercises make this one of the best industry books I've read in a long time."

—Holli Catchpole, President
SpeakersOffice, Inc.

"Wow! At last, a step-by-step guide for success in the speaking business — no need to be reinventing the wheel as Jane reveals the secrets to success. This book is a must read if you're serious about super-charging your career."

— Kit Grant, Former World President
International Federation for Professional Speakers

"I have been in the speaking business for over 22 years and I can honestly say that *The Wealthy Speaker* is one of the best resources I have ever found. Follow the advice in this book and it will help you take your speaking career to the next level."

—Dr. Brad McRae, CSP, Platinum Level Presenter MPI

THE Wealthy SPEAKER 2.0

The **Proven Formula**
for building your
successful speaking business

Jane Atkinson

First Printing

Library and Archives Canada Cataloguing in Publication

Atkinson, Jane, 1964-

    The wealthy speaker 2.0 : the proven formula for building your successful speaking business / Jane Atkinson. — 2nd ed.

Issued also in electronic format.

ISBN 978-0-9780059-8-6

1. Public speaking—Vocational guidance. I. Title.

PN4098.A85 2012   808.5'1023   C2012-904351-6

Editor: Catherine Leek of Green Onion Publishing
Electronic Page Composition: Kim Monteforte, WeMakeBooks.ca
Front Cover Design: Tim Handleman
Back Cover Design: Beth Crane, WeMakeBooks.ca
Cartoons: Steve Morris

Printed in USA.

Contents

• •

Chapter 4: Phase II: Aim

Foreword

● ●

There's an old saying: "We don't get hurt by what we don't know. We get hurt by what we know but don't do." After you read *The Wealthy Speaker 2.0* — you will know. You will know how to begin your speaking career or reenergize your existing one. You will know the importance of keeping your strategies and tactics in alignment with your true strengths and personal motivations. And you will know how to become a "wealthy speaker" in the broadest sense of the word — not just in the quantity of money you create, but in terms of the quality of the career you create. Then it's a matter of taking action.

The value of this book is found in the quality of its content. Beyond data, facts and information about the speaking profession, Jane delivers that rare commodity of wisdom. There's no shortcut to wisdom. You have to pay your dues, make lots of bad decisions and learn a lot of painful lessons to get to the point where you finally know what you're doing. Even then, if you are truly wise, you keep growing. Jane has been there and done that. She's seen the speaking business from a number of perspectives and has learned and grown every step of the way. You will have to travel your own path to wisdom, but having this book with you as you make the journey will be of immeasurable value.

At the National Speakers Association annual convention a few years ago, I gave a keynote speech about the power of being willing to let go. After thirty years in this business, I still believe that the most important thing I can do to keep my career growing is to always be willing to let go of my assumptions and embrace new ideas.

The business of speaking has changed more in the past five years than it did in the previous twenty-five. Technology, social media, and shifts in the economy have made it more important than ever to have a new perspective about how you spend your money and your time. *The Wealthy Speaker 2.0* helps you strategize to use these changes to your advantage.

As you read this book, I challenge you to let go of any preconceived ideas you may have about your speaking career. Be open and willing to learn from Jane and the fabulous speaking professionals who have contributed to this book.

For many years, when any speaker has asked me for advice on what they can do to take their career to the next level, I have replied, "Let me start with three words: Call Jane Atkinson." To that advice I will now add five more words: "Read *The Wealthy Speaker 2.0*."

Joe Calloway, CSP, CPAE
Author of *Becoming a Category of One*

A Day in the Life of a Wealthy Speaker

Imagine that you are having the perfect day in your life as a professional speaker. You are standing in front of your ideal audience. You had them at "hello" and you rocked it all the way through until the closing. As you exit the stage to thunderous applause, the leader of the organization meets you backstage and pumps your hand. "Thank you so much. That was exactly what our people needed to hear! I've got some great ideas for our next consulting call. I'll be in touch."

Laurie, the meeting coordinator, comes to escort you over to your autograph session. She's giddy over the response and hands you a check for the remainder of your fee — $15,000. You thank her and let her know that your office will send the travel expenses, which they'd gladly agreed to ahead of time — first-class all the way.

You engage with your audience at the autograph session where you sign a few hundred pre-purchased books and take photos with audience members to post on Twitter. It's two hours, but a really great experience that nets an additional $4,000 in product sales. Laurie returns to take you to your limo and Charlie, your driver, has your bag in the trunk ready to go. He knows you from the last few times this client has hired you and asks how your day went.

Once in the car, you call your fabulous assistant, who tells you that he has secured three more engagements. Woo hoo! One of the engagements is in Hawaii and the client has agreed to two first-class tickets and wants to know if you'd like to bring your spouse and stay an extra few days after the event. Ahhhh, yeah! He also informs you that your publishing partner called and they are bumping up the PR and social media budget on your next (fourth) book. The editor from the *Wall Street Journal* also left word that they are considering you for their lead story.

When you arrive home, your loving spouse greets you with a long, lingering kiss. You have a special getaway planned for the upcoming weekend.

Your home office has run smoothly and efficiently while you were away. And when you return, you deal only with high-level decisions, writing and product development, relationships with clients, and joint venture partners. The rest of your time is focused on family and play.

Bzzzzzz.

What's that annoying sound? Your alarm clock is waking you from this wonderful dream. That was a good dream! Is it possible to achieve this dream for yourself? Absolutely. It's going to take some work and you'll need to create your own vision, but it is possible.

THE WEALTHY
SPEAKER PREMISE

Reality Bites

The reality of the speaking business is that it's not nearly as glamorous as the previous scenario. Chances are that one of your flights will be delayed or canceled. You might be sick to death of traveling and miss your family terribly. You might have a two-year-old with a cold and you cry all the way to the airport. I've seen this happen!

You could potentially bomb on stage — all speakers have bombed at some point. And your family — if they are like most — will never truly understand what it is that you do for a living. And they will secretly wish — no matter how successful you become — that you would get a *real* job. The bottom line is that this business is not all standing ovations and juicy paychecks. The 30 minutes that you get to bask in the limelight after a standing O could easily turn into 30 hours of travel nightmare.

So, let's be realistic about this decision and get clear on your motivation. (See My Motivation in Chapter 2.)

2.0   **FLASHPOINT: Ryan Estis**

In January of 2009 our country suffered its worst job loss in 34 years. My industry was no exception. The economy was in sharp decline and it was clear we were heading into the worst recession since the great depression. The future was anything but certain.

I was fortunate. I had built up 17 years of equity in the advertising and communications industry. As the Chief Sales and Strategy Officer for a division of a well respected, international agency my role was pretty secure. It was exactly during this moment that I decided security was no longer something I coveted.

In February of 2009 I launched Ryan Estis & Associates. My speaking enterprise was born. My timing couldn't have been worse, or so I was told. I had been delivering industry-related keynotes and break-out sessions as part of my corporate role for a few years. That experience and exposure to speaking helped give me the confidence to take my shot.

I will never forget the first time someone asked me how much I charged to speak. Charge?! It was about that time I started to conduct research. I joined the National Speakers Association, participated in the graduate and apprenticeship programs, read the first edition of this book, and hired the author as my coach. I put in the time and made the investment to really understand the business of professional speaking.

I learned there are a million different approaches to the platform and world of professional speaking. People speak to promote their consulting business. People speak to generate an alternative revenue stream. People speak to earn a second income.

However, most of those people aren't likely to become a Wealthy Speaker.

For me that was and remains the goal.

Speaking is my business. My third year into the business we are starting to see growth and realizing that objective. Through a combination of keynote speeches and training engagements our business will more than double year over year and we are fortunate to count some of the largest companies in the world as clients.

In hindsight starting at the bottom was a blessing in disguise. Any sense of corporate entitlement quickly washed away with the harsh realization of waking each day to the kitchen table, laptop, and a telephone that wasn't going to ring. Running a speaking business is a sales and marketing play. I never counted on third party partnerships to build my business. While they are valued today, you have to know how to sell yourself first before anyone else can succeed selling for you. I have scheduled selling time built into my calendar every week. In the beginning the vast majority of my time was spent on sales.

While the barrier to entry and fixed capital costs to start a speaking business are low, it still needs to run like a business. That means establishing a budget and a business plan with specific and measurable objectives. You need to invest to compete — that means a website, video, marketing resources, tools, technology, and eventually a key contributor (staff person) who can keep the business running when you are developing content or delivering for customers. I believe understanding this from the outset has been a key competitive advantage and helped accelerate our growth.

My secret to success is there isn't a secret. It is demanding. It is competitive. I know that for every engagement I deliver there are a thousand other competent and capable speakers who could do the same. Every opportunity to impact a client is a gift that I never take for granted. Being a good speaker is no longer good enough. Today, you have to excel in every facet of the business — speaking, writing, curriculum design, marketing, sales, and customer service.

It is an enormous challenge but there is an abundance of opportunity. We are living through a period of accelerated transformation and change. New ideas, insights, and breakthrough thinking will always be in high demand. For the speaker who is relevant, can deliver ideas that inspire action, and impact results, the sky is the limit.

I cannot imagine anything that is more fun ... or rewarding!

So What Exactly is a Wealthy Speaker?

Success is subjective. One speaker's successful year might not appeal to another speaker at all. So it's up to you to decide what success looks like for you. You might only want to speak once a month at a fee of $15,000 or you might want to speak ten times per month at $1,500. Every speaker has his or her own set of goals and no one can dictate your goals but you. What I can do, as your coach, is make sure that you are thinking big. After living in Texas for six years, I learned how to think bigger.

Will you have to work hard to get to a $15,000 fee? You bet you will, but it's not impossible. Sometimes one major speaking engagement like the Million Dollar Round Table (MDRT), Meeting Professionals International (MPI), or a major industry conference in your target market can change the course of a speaker's career. Or it might be a book that hits the bestseller list or creates a lot of excitement. I've seen things change overnight — but it was years of hard work that led up to the turning point or what we call Flashpoints (see later in this chapter).

"Success occurs when preparation meets opportunity."
— Henry Hartman

Ryan's story is a terrific example of someone who is doing the right things in order to create opportunities. He may have steady growth for several years and then see a major flashpoint when he speaks at a large industry conference or publishes his first book. As Henry Hartman says, "Success occurs when preparation meets opportunity."

2.0 THE INDUSTRY: YESTERDAY AND TODAY

When I was five years into my career as a speaker's agent, we were in our heyday. At the time, none of us realized that this was what we would later refer to as "the good old days." In the good old days, a speaker could go from 0 to 80 engagements a year in three years. Can that still happen? Well, in fact it can still happen (see Flashpoint: Ryan Estis earlier in this chapter), but it's not nearly as common as it used to be.

Much has changed since I first wrote *The Wealthy Speaker* in 2005. With the economic meltdown of 2008, U.S. Congress starting looking into the books of companies they were bailing out. Under that public scrutiny, corporations and associations were compelled to justify their spending. Prior to that, similar events such as 9/11 and the SARS epidemic saw some speakers' entire calendars wiped clean.

Today, we brace ourselves for knee jerk reactions by the corporate decision makers. On several occasions, they have rocked the travel and meeting industries, as well as the speaking world.

Every time the economy shifts, corporate leaders get nervous and meetings get pushed back or canceled. An industry that once saw speakers being booked 15 months out, now sees bookings with 2-3-week lead times. Although it makes it difficult to plan, I have to say, this may make more sense. If you are a corporate leader who wants to be on the cutting edge, you want to book speakers who are timely and relevant and that may not be possible when booking a year in advance.

> *An industry that once saw speakers being booked 15 months out, now sees bookings with 2-3-week lead times.*

According to statistics of NSA (National Speakers Association), our industry continues to have a lot of newcomers and, when bunched in with the seasoned speakers, the average earnings are around $125,000 for speaking and $132,000 for product sales. The males in our industry earn a higher average fee than females, which is pretty annoying if you ask me. (Ladies, a good place to start ... is demanding what we're worth!)

Our industry now has a very small percentage (1%, down from 3%) of speakers who are earning over $1 million per year in total revenues. And those are the speakers we're talking about when we use the phrase "The Wealthy Speaker." Our goal is not to aim for average! I've added several more Flashpoints to this 2.0 Version to show you that, even in an appalling economy, you can still be "A Wealthy Speaker!" Not all, but many, of the Flashpoint stories you'll read are from speakers who fall into this top 1% category and there are several from speakers who are well on their way.

> *Even in an appalling economy, you can still be "A Wealthy Speaker!"*

Sales Sidebar

Notice that we have "pull quotes" of various phrases that bring important thoughts to the forefront. Well, what am I doing here? Typically, I'm quoting myself. I could quote Winston Churchill or some other famous person, but when I quote myself, I become the expert in your mind. When you are writing your book, giving speeches, and designing your website, be sure to quote yourself.

2.0 SO WHAT ELSE IS NEW?

Aside from the economic shifts in the past years, technology has also shifted our business. We are faced with social media dilemmas, new technologies arriving daily (for the platform and the business), new marketing opportunities, and clients who continually want more for less. Starting any small business now can be overwhelming and that's why the Ready, Aim, Fire approach is going to help you move through it smoothly. (See Ready, Aim, Fire in Chapter 2).

Because of the economic shifts, today we want to expand from simply being a "speaker" to being an expert who speaks. Speaking is simply one way to distribute our knowledge. We might have books, webinars, membership clubs, online training programs, etc., that help compliment our speaking.

I call this umbrella (see Figure A) your empire. And this is your empire to build as big or small as you like. My advice, for those who want to become truly wealthy in money terms, however, is that you build a bustling empire with several revenue streams — not just speaking.

BUT WHAT IF I'M JUST STARTING OUT?

You'll probably look at these numbers and think they are unattainable, but let me reassure you that every speaker, no matter how successful, started with zero engagements on his or her calendar at one point in time. Allow yourself to dream, to shoot for just a little more than you think is possible. Stretch!

When using the Umbrella (see Figure A), try to work on one revenue stream at a time. If you try to launch a book, a keynote career, and a membership club all in the same year, I think you'll be overwhelmed. Each one of those is like starting a new small business. So treat them that way. When you launch a new product, treat it like a new business and put everything you have behind it for a period of time.

FIGURE A: **Umbrella**

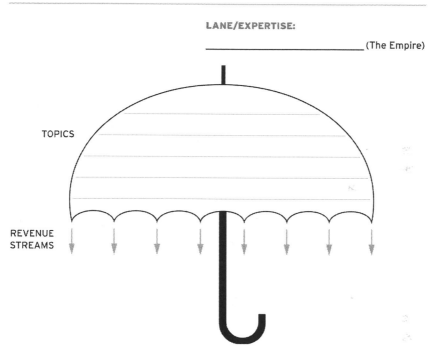

This umbrella (your business model) will help you stay focused. First fill in the top line with your focused topic area. This is an internal document, so you could write in something broad like "Leadership Communication." After that, in the body of the umbrella, place your speech and book titles. Examples might be "Communication for Leaders," "Communication for Healthy Teams." Then using the arrows at the bottom, list your revenue streams. That might be keynotes, workshops, retreats, books, webinars.

STEPPING UP

It takes courage to move into this business from any other profession. There is a huge learning curve, not a lot of security, and you must have a higher than average level of confidence. But are you going to let fear get in your way? Most decisions based on fear are usually wrong.

Most decisions based on fear are usually wrong.

Think about the kind of person you will need to become to fully step into life as a professional speaker. You will need to be a courageous leader. If you know that you have a strong, original message for the world and that you are a great speaker, then step up. Do not let fear come between you and what you want. Do not play small. Coaching Exercise 2, A Day in Your Life Five Years from Now (a little later in this chapter), will help you gain some clarity around what you want in the future. But today, as a speaker and as a leader, you must step boldly into your greatness.

Start a file or an e-mail folder labeled "Genius." Place copies of your best client testimonials and positive feedback you have received in the file. You might even write a letter to yourself with some positive reinforcements. Then, on the tough days, when you wonder what the heck you are doing in this career, pull out your Genius file and go through it. It will remind you why you started this journey in the first place.

The speaking industry needs committed people who are in it for the right reasons. If you are unsure or uncommitted, then you must reconsider.

Start-Up Speaker's Quiz

Starting up a speaking business is the same as starting any business. So you must do your homework and prepare. Coaching Exercise 1 contains some questions that will allow you to assess where you are in the process. If this quiz scares the *pants off you, good*! You need to do more work before you start or perhaps you might re-evaluate.

Coaching Exercise 1: START-UP SPEAKER'S QUIZ

Starting up a speaking business is the same as starting any business. So you must do your homework and prepare.

Ask yourself the following questions and answer with complete honesty. After all, if you can't be honest with yourself, who can you be honest with?

1. Have I done my research? What do I know about this business? What do I need to learn?

    _____

    _____

    _____

2. Is there a demand for what I offer? How many speakers are making a living doing something similar?

    _____

    _____

3. How much cash do I have set aside to launch my business?

    _____

    _____

4. Can I support a negative cash flow? For how many months?

    _____

    _____

5. Is this really what I want? Why? Am I ready now?

    _____

    _____

6. Is my speech prepared? Do I know the return on investment for the audience?

    _____

    _____

7. Is my family willing to support this?

   _____

   _____

8. How am I, or how is my message, different from that of my competition?

   _____

   _____

9. Do I know who my competition is?

   _____

   _____

10. Am I good enough to go the distance? Have people from within the industry (and people who could hire me) told me that?

    _____

    _____

11. Am I an entrepreneur? Do I know how to run a business?

    _____

    _____

12. Am I confident enough?

    _____

    _____

13. Do I have a solid business plan?

    _____

    _____

14. What will my banker and my accountant say?

    _____

    _____

Bonus Questions

15. Is my topic relevant and timely?

_____

_____

16. How much do I know about technology and can I learn what I need to know?

_____

_____

17. Am I prepared to do what it takes to leap into business in today's climate?

_____

_____

18. Is your family situation (children) set up so that you can focus on your career when you need to? Do you have the support you need?

_____

_____

If you answered negatively or were unsure about the majority of these questions, you might have some homework to do prior to starting this process. You might even decide that you don't want to move ahead. But if you answered positively to the majority, then we are ready to proceed. But don't think the tough questions are over — there are lots more where these came from.

You can also find all of these exercises in a separate and conveniently bound workbook: *Wealthy Speaker Workbook and Planning Guide.*

The Wealthy Speaker Mind-Set

A huge part of the wealthy speaker equation is being able to accept wealth into your life. You need to condition for success. If you've been successful in other fields, then this isn't going to be much of a challenge for you, but if you've always struggled with building wealth and abundance, then you will continue to struggle unless you change your mind-set.

RECONDITION YOUR THOUGHT PATTERNS

Vince Poscente shared an analogy many years ago that has stuck with me. Being an Olympic athlete, he studied the power of the mind. He told me that our thoughts are like a river that has been traveling the same route through a valley for many years. The rock and land have been worn away creating the path of least resistance. The water will continue on this path forever unless diverted. The river represents your thought patterns. Basically, you think the way you've always thought. Perhaps you don't believe that you deserve to be wealthy or you can't possibly buy into the fact that you don't need to work your fingers to the bone in order to earn a nice living.

If you were raised like me, the conversations often included phrases like "money doesn't grow on trees" along with numerous other sayings that lacked positive enforcement. These sayings and attitudes helped build the river of your thoughts in the first place. But then you grow up and attend a seminar by Anthony Robbins or Tim Ferris and you make a decision. "That's it, I'm going to be wealthy. No more messing around." You start the process, but your river continues to take you through the same valley and you find yourself staying in the same state of struggle. So what do you do?

You need to recondition your mind as though you are training for a marathon. To return to the river analogy, you are building a dam in order to reroute the water. So how do you do this? There are many different methods you can use and many great books on the subject of shifting your mind-set. Two of my favorite books are Wayne Dyer's *Power of Intention* and Eric Butterworth's *Spiritual Economics*. You'll find them listed on The Wealthy Speaker website. One of my favorite reconditioning methods is relaxation tapes. Listening to positive statements about wealth over and over can start to build the dam and reroute your thought patterns toward something more positive.

2.0 ASK BETTER QUESTIONS

My personal experience has allowed me to shift my mind-set several times over the past decade. But when I was turning 40 (several years ago) it dawned on me that I was still playing small. I realized that all the people that I represented were making a healthy six figures and I was not. So I made a decision to stop limiting myself. Why shouldn't I go for that $400K house by the river? I began asking myself the question: Who do I need to become? As it turns out, "an author" was the answer to that question. And after writing *The Wealthy Speaker* back in 2005, I was able to afford that house by the river.

Asking great questions is the key to achieving your goals. The question "How can I get a million dollars?" won't hold the same power as "What haven't I thought of yet?"

In order to start rerouting the river's path in your mind, you need to be able to identify the new path. You need to know what your wealth or your success will look like. Try Coaching Exercise 2, A Day in Your Life Five Years from Now, a little further along in this chapter. It is important to know what your Wealthy Speaker day will look like. We'll refer back to this image many times. Remember — think big!

> **WEBSITE REFERENCE TOOL**
>
> **www.speakerlauncher.com** ➡
> **Book Buyer LOGIN** *(red button)*
>
> **Recommended Reading:** Wayne Dyer, *Power of Intention*; Eric Butterworth, *Spiritual Economics*; Tim Ferris, *The Four Hour Work Week*.

2.0 LIFESTYLE BUSINESS

The Wealthy Speaker Lifestyle is not necessarily one of private jets and limos. It's actually more of a mentality that leads your business decisions. Creating a lifestyle business is designing a life that allows you to do all of the things that you want to do each day and none of the things that you hate — and generating enough income to afford you those choices.

I remember several years ago Tom Antion was talking about how his computer would make the sound of a cash register every time a sale came in. Making money while sleeping, yes! So I set out to create the vision of my perfect business. What did this look like?

After reading Tim Ferris' book, *The Four Hour Work Week*, I realized I didn't want to be tied to the business. This is why I moved away from managing speakers — you couldn't take off for two weeks when meeting planners and executives wanted to talk to you about your speaker. You worked to their timelines. It also means that I can operate my business simply with a laptop. My calls come in through my computer when I'm at my cottage for two weeks in the summer time and in Florida for two or more weeks in the winter. I've designed it so I can now work from anywhere.

Travel has always been a goal for me, but because I'm newly married (five years now; I still consider it new), I don't want to be gone from home unless my husband comes with me. Therefore, I accept no more than eight engagements a year, four in the Spring, four in the Fall — mostly to groups of speakers — which don't pay well, but successfully feed all of my revenue streams. And my husband does come with me when it's a location on his bucket list. We've been lucky to explore New York, San Francisco, Vancouver, Halifax, Dallas and New Orleans in the past couple of years.

So that I'm not always trading my time for money, I have a whole host of products and online sales have become a big part of my revenue strategy. Also, if I ever got sick, I hope these would help pay the bills.

I also decided that I didn't want to work every day of the week, so Fridays have become my day off. Since I don't have much brain power left after 4 P.M., coaching from 11-3 is the schedule. You might wonder if my clients complain about this, but I'm teaching them to build the business of their dreams, so they understand.

What's perfect for you? Here are a few questions that can help you.

- How can I make money without trading it for my time?
- How much travel do I want to do?
- How can I translate my knowledge into new products?
- How much time do I want to spend away from my office and how can I make this seamless?
- What are the priorities in my life that come before my business (i.e., health, family, etc.)?

Coaching Exercise 2: A DAY IN YOUR LIFE FIVE YEARS FROM NOW

You may want to type out this exercise and save it. We'll be referring back to it a few times. But once you're finished, you can post it somewhere prominent and look at it regularly. Olympic athletes swear by visualization exercises and, since they make it to the Olympics, I guess they must work!

Go back to A Day in the Life of a Wealthy Speaker (page xix) and read it again. Look at the verbs used … present tense. Now write down what your perfect day looks like five years from now. Put down all of the details. Who do you speak for? Or consult with? At what fee? What are the results? How does that feel? What type of audience is it? What do your home and office life look like? Do you have a vacation house? Where is it? How much time do you spend there? Where else do you go for vacation? Do you have product? What are your passive income streams? What do your personal relationships look like? What kind of fun are you and your family having? Are you healthy?

Don't leave out any detail — this is your perfect day.

Once you have completed the exercise, place it in a prominent place and review it daily. Make it a part of your morning ritual. Allow the principle of "you become what you think about most of the time" to work in your favor.

_____

_____

_____

_____

_____

_____

_____

_____

_____

_____

_____

_____

_____

_____

_____

_____

_____

_____

_____

_____

_____

_____

_____

_____

_____

_____

_____

_____

_____

_____

_____

_____

_____

_____

_____

IMAGINE THE POSSIBILITIES

I went to work for an up-and-coming speaker and former Olympic speed skier named Vince Poscente in the summer of 1996. It was my first day on the job in Dallas, TX, and the thermometer hit 95°F as I pulled up to our office at 9 a.m. We shared office space with Vince's girlfriend, Michelle, who owned International Speakers Bureau. Part of the reason I accepted this job was because I thought I could learn a lot working under the roof of a speakers' bureau. Michelle had four employees at the time and her business was growing rapidly. On Vince's side, it was just the two of us. Vince and I got together for our first strategy meeting and I asked to see the booking board — I wanted to see how many gigs we had for the next few months. We went into his office to look at the giant 12-month wall calendar and it hit me — we had no business! There were one or two engagements, each confirmed at $2,500. "Yikes," I thought. "What have I gotten myself into?" I had left a very successful, multi-millionaire speaker in Vancouver to work with Vince. It was a big risk on both of our parts. As I stood there in stunned silence wondering if I'd made a huge mistake, I remembered something that Michelle had said to me during my five-day job interview (details on this in Chapter 7 under Hiring Staff Who are Winners). She said, "Vince will work as hard on his speech as he did to get to the Olympics."

Vince and I went to lunch that day to do some goal setting. Over burgers and beer, we talked about where we saw this company going. I asked Vince what fee he would like to see us aspire to — I used the term "us" because Vince and I had agreed that we were partners in this. He shrugged. So I said, "How about $10,000?" He paused for a moment and said, "Okay." We set two other major goals: we wanted to get him booked into a national Meeting Professionals International (MPI) meeting; and we would get him on the main platform at Million Dollar Round Table (MDRT). We went back to the office and posted those three items on my bulletin board and went to work. Vince had used the power of his mind to get to the Olympics and we used some of those techniques to reach our goals. More importantly, he worked his butt off making the speech really great. And I worked my butt off marketing him to meeting planners and speakers' bureaus. It took a long time for the speakers' bureaus to book Vince because they were worried that we would share the clients with Michelle's company. We went above and beyond to ensure that our integrity was never questioned and bureaus ended up being 80% of our business.

Our hard work paid off. We went back to the board after three years and realized we had met all three goals. Vince's fee was $10,000, he was speaking 80+ times per year, and he had spoken at both MPI and MDRT. We were ecstatic.

Fast forward another two years. It's the National Speakers Association (NSA) convention in New Orleans, and Vince has just been awarded both his CSP and CPAE* Awards. He could have had his CSP a lot earlier, but I had always given him the choice of my time being spent getting bookings or doing the (then) huge amount of paperwork to get his CSP. He always chose the bookings! Anyway, we were out in the hallway after the ceremony. Vince's fee had risen another 50% at this point and he was still doing 80+ bookings per year. He said to me, "You know that day, when we set our goals over beer and burgers?" I said I remembered. He said, "When you suggested $10,000 I really thought you were smoking something. I really couldn't imagine my fee going there." I was shocked. He had never told me that he had any doubt at all, but he had used his own techniques, the power of the mind, to grow into the idea that it was possible. Once he broke the barrier, there was no stopping him. (See Vince's Flashpoint Update in Phase I: Ready.)

> **WEBSITE REFERENCE TOOL**
>
> www.speakerlauncher.com ➡
> Book Buyer LOGIN *(red button)*
> **Recommended Reading:** *Taming Your Gremlin* by Rick Carson available on Amazon.com

So how does this affect you? When you are writing your five-year vision, make sure that you are not letting your gremlin (the little green man on your shoulder that says "Are you crazy? That's not possible! Who are you kidding?") put limits on your goals. Don't let the gremlin drive the bus. Be in charge of setting the goals you want to create — don't hold back.

Go back through your five-year vision and make sure that you aren't playing small.

---

*CSP (Certified Speaking Professional) and CPAE (Council of Peers Award of Excellence) are NSA designations. A very small group of speakers have both.

How to Spend Your Time, Energy, and Money

Throughout this book you will find tons of ideas for things you should be doing — from developing the speech, to building marketing materials, to setting and raising fees, to working with bureaus, to hiring staff, to setting up your office with systems, to developing product. Yikes! That could be overwhelming no matter what stage of your career you are in. Stop and take a good look at Figure B. No matter where you are in your career, you'll get some clarity around where you should best spend your time and resources. This should take off some pressure to do everything today!

FIGURE B: **Focus Areas**

Experience	Years Speaking	Area of Focus
New Speakers	Years 0–3	The Speech – make it good!
		Positioning in the market as an expert
		Building marketing materials that represent you (they may not be perfect)
		Building your social media platform
		Developing relationships with clients — getting your name out there
		Pulling people into your team who might help you get there (part time, virtual)
Seasoned Speakers	Years 4–6	The Speech — keep working it!
		Getting your marketing to the next level (now it needs to be good)
		Repositioning, if necessary
		Continuing to grow your social media platform and ensure you are converting some to clients
		Building on your reputation (which means moving your fee up the ladder)

Experience	Years Speaking	Area of Focus
		Product Development — full steam ahead (some people may launch into the business with a book, and that's great too)
		Developing systems in your office — you'll need them now
		Building the team (staff — part time or full time) and making inroads with speakers' bureaus (work the business yourself for a few years before doing this)
Mature Speakers	Years 7+	The Speech — keep it fresh and fun for you — Reinvent it!
		Marketing and social media — update (don't get complacent)
		Reposition if necessary — new products, new markets — stay cutting edge
		Continue with long-term relationship building — keep your name out there in fresh ways
		By now your office should run like a well oiled machine

About the Book's Aids and Tools

Throughout this book, you'll find special features highlighted to assist you in becoming a Wealthy Speaker. Overall the goal is an easy, yet thought-provoking, read. These features will provide additional sources of information and inspiration or challenge your preconceived ideas. Here is the list of features so that you can watch for them or seek them out specifically.

Coach's Question: *The coach's question will help you focus on some of your main goals. It will pose a question or two and provide some feedback on what you will need to think about in order to gain the most from the information.*

Sales Sidebars

These are like insider trading only not illegal. I'm modeling specific sales strategies for you while writing this book, but in this case, I'm telling you how I am selling you while I'm doing it so that you can learn to do it for yourself. Call me an evil genius, but I think transparency is the best way to teach and sell at the same time! I do this in my presentations as well. (See, this is me planting the seed that I speak, and when you have a group that needs to know about becoming a Wealthy Speaker, you might think of me. Two birds.)

COACHING EXERCISES

You will find numerous exercises to complete as you move through the book — if you haven't already completed two, go back to the beginning of this chapter. These are meant for you to use — perhaps several times — as your focus or your goals change.

WEBSITE REFERENCE TOOL

I've set up some special pages for you under the "Book Buyer Login" section of my website. There you will find a resource for speakers and suppliers who are mentioned in the book, along with some special offers. This website will not only be a wealth of information for you, but my blog and social media sites may become a great place for you to seek advice and share ideas with people. Go to www.speakerlauncher.com and click on Book Buyer LOGIN *(red button)*.

For your convenience the exercises can also be found in the companion workbook, *Wealthy Speaker Workbook and Planning Guide.* Note: 2.0 Bonus Questions are not in the workbook at this time.

FLASHPOINT: Flashpoints in a Wealthy
Speaker's Career

You are going to see examples of the most significant and
pivotal points in a speaker's career — I call them Flashpoints, a
term I've borrowed from Vince Poscente. You'll see what
helped them take the leap to the next level. There are usually
several years of hard work prior to Flashpoints, but they are a
great learning tool for speakers who are just starting out or
who want to jump a level. Watch for the lightning bolt symbol
that indicates a Flashpoint story. They are typcially first-hand
accounts from the speaker.

2.0 UPDATES

You'll see throughout the book, there are some bonus 2.0 coach's
questions, flashpoints, and 2.0 updates. These, in conjunction with
some updates to information in other sections, are additions that
were made to ensure that this book is as current as possible. Of
course, I realize that the minute I stop writing, the book will once
again be out of date! It's a process.

MY PROMISE TO YOU

I got into the speaking industry as a booking agent for a speaker
more than 20 years ago and I feel lucky to be a part of something so
important. Some of the world's greatest minds are in our industry
and some of the most thought-provoking, inspirational people walk
the halls of our industry events. They are out there making the world
a better place with their messages. Our business has its ups and
downs, but knowledge is power. The more you know, the more you
can compete when the market dips and thrive when the market peaks.
I want you to be armed with the best equipment a speaker can have
— information, ideas, and powerful questions. I'll be your personal
coach, walking you through the formula step by step. And I won't be
far away if you need support when you're finished.

It is probably well documented (somewhere) that the majority of
self-help and business book purchasers buy a book expecting it will

change their lives. They read a small number of pages and then put it into their bedside table where it sits with the other six books … forgotten.

Sales Sidebar

I'm driving you to my website to see all of these cool tools for a reason. Why? I want you to be familiar with my website so that when you are ready to advance to the next steps, and need some help, I'll be familiar to you. What are you doing in your books to drive people to your website?

If Figure C is the only page you read, read this page. The odds of you reading the entire book go up 500%* if you know what you will miss by not reading past this page of the book.

FIGURE C: **Overview**

	What You'll Find	Who It's Best Suited For
Chapter 1	What is a Wealthy Speaker and what foundation do I need to have in place to become one?	Speakers at all levels, unless you already earn $1,000,000 per year. Then you can just use this book as a doorstop.
Chapter 2	Preparing for launch. Take the time to design the business that you desire using the Ready, Aim, Fire, approach. Don't miss this!	Speakers at all levels, especially the speaker who has tried lots of things, but isn't quite "making it" yet.
Chapter 3	Focus on which topic will bring you the most success, position yourself as the expert, and put together a great speech.	Every speaker should be working on improving his or her speech … always. Good stuff here.

---

*Okay, I made that number up.

	What You'll Find	Who It's Best Suited For
Chapter 4	Develop marketing materials and Social Media platforms that will result in bookings. What works, what does not.	All speakers. Many will be tempted to start this book here. But don't do it. Respect the process.
Chapter 5	Find the business, do the outreach and, build a database. Book the gigs!	Feel free to skip this section if you don't need any more speaking engagements.
Chapter 6	Speakers' Bureaus are a world onto themselves. Get the inside scoop.	You need to build your own contacts first, but after a few years you should be ready for Speakers' Bureaus.
Chapter 7	Develop new products, hire staff, set up systems, and use technology.	All speakers. Same as Chapter 5.
Being a Super Hero	Final thoughts, a little pep talk to send you on your way.	Well, you've read the rest, why stop now?

2

GETTING READY TO LAUNCH

My Motivation

• •

Coach's Question: *Why do I want to be a speaker? What is really motivating this career choice?*

If you answer, "because I have a message that I need to share" then you might have something. You might also be on the right track if you have a strong business background and/or some unique expertise that could benefit your audiences. Any number of reasons could motivate you to get into this business. However, if you were sitting in the audience one day and saw a speaker and thought, "Hey that looks cool, I think I'll give that a shot," then you might have to stop and reassess. Your passion for your expertise is what will pull you through the tough times, so if you start out with none, you'll be reading the help wanted ads at the first sign of stress. Be sure about your motivation and be committed to the long-term process.

> *It takes 3 to 5 years to get a successful speaking business launched.*

FLASHPOINT: Toni Newman

When I came into the speaking business, I thought I was going to be different. After all, I was coming from a solid business background and, although I was new to the speaking industry, I had been speaking to groups for years about Creativity in Business — the core specialty that I intended to build my speaking business around. I nodded politely and smiled when everyone from coaches and mentors to colleagues and friends told me that it would take at least three years to get my business off the ground — because inside I knew I had an edge. I knew I was going to be different.

Boy — was I in for a surprise!

Yes, I had run a successful business for ten years and, yes, I knew what needed to be done to recreate that success. But knowing isn't enough. You have to be able to put what you know into action — alone! No more employees to help breath life into my crazy ideas. No more suppliers to help with the day-to-day tasks. Now the buck started and stopped with me!

Not only had my business reality changed, my personal reality had changed as well. I was now the proud mother of two children under four years of age, no longer the 100-hour-a-week workaholic that I had been when my husband and I launched our first company ten years earlier. Now family needed to come first. I quickly made the choice not to work evenings or weekends so that I could find balance in my life — still planning to get my business off to this amazing quicker than life start, of course.

Business was okay but not great and money was tight all-round. I beat myself up a lot during those first years, constantly worrying about whether or not I really had the dedication required to start a new speaking business. However, I managed to keep my eye on my goals and stay focused on my expertise. At times I was tempted to accept work outside of my area but I knew that would do more harm than good, so I hung in. Then, suddenly, the business turned a corner and the engagements literally started to pour in.

As I look back, I realize that dedication to a business comes in all shapes and sizes. I've learned that the best competitive edge is focus and there is no way around the fact that developing focus requires insight and that accumulating that insight just takes time!

I recently won my first long-term contract and the engagements continue to come in. I reach my target number of full-fee keynotes per month most of the time and the bulk of my business comes from referrals and past participants. My total revenue for this year will hit six figures but, as everyone predicted, it's taken me three years to get here.

Hey, it looks like I'm not so different after all!

 ## 2.0 TONI NEWMAN

As I re-read what I wrote for *The Wealthy Speaker* over five years ago, I was struck by one thing — not that much has changed.

I still believe that laser-like focus in terms of your area of expertise is the best competitive advantage that any of us can have. Staying true to who you are and what you know may not always be easy — particularly when there is pressure all around us to embark on a "hot topic" or take advantage of "a great opportunity" — but it has paid off for me and I believe that it can pay off for you.

However, there was an added bonus to my "fanatical focus" that I didn't anticipate back when I first wrote for *The Wealthy Speaker*. Simply put, as the depth of my expertise has grown, so has the depth of the relationships that I am able to cultivate with my clients. When someone comes knocking on your door because you have knowledge that is of value to them, terrific opportunities for conversations about the best way to deliver that knowledge are created. And after all, isn't that why we're in this business in the first place? To create something new and unique that delivers value?

So here I am five years later. My business has evolved from primarily keynotes to a myriad of delivery methods where the possibilities are endless. I am less preoccupied with short-term events and more excited about long-term opportunities. I am still fanatical about fee integrity but I've stopped pricing myself like a speaker. I took my eye off the ball once and the universe kicked my butt. I won't let that happen again.

I have a great family. I have a great business. And lucky me … almost every day I learn something new that I can use to make a difference in the lives of the people around me.

So … maybe a few things have changed after all!

MOTIVATIONAL? INSPIRATIONAL? TOPICAL?

We all have definitions for the difference between motivation and inspiration — I'll give you mine. Inspiration is when your audience is inspired by a story. Often it's a personal story like my client Paul Templer who's arm was bitten off by a hippopotamus — okay, that's not so typical. He talks about how he survived the attack and then overcame severe depression afterwards to go on to lead a fulfilling life. It's a survival story. Then there is Scott Burrows, who is one of the few quadriplegics to walk again — it took him six years. His audiences are completely inspired. And there are many of you out there who live your lives or overcome obstacles in an inspiring manner.

Then there's motivation. Motivation often has a strategy or formula. Vince Poscente's motivational message includes the 5 C formula that helped him get to the Olympics in an incredibly short period of time. People get something they can take away and apply to their own lives.

But then there are all of the speakers who don't fit into the motivational/inspirational category. They speak on topics like leadership, branding, retail, dentistry, etc. They don't speak about personal tragedies, the mountains they've climbed or going to the Olympics, but they make up a huge percentage of the Wealthy Speaker population. Why? They have an expertise that the corporate world or association markets will pay to hear. They know stuff other people don't know or they have a new spin or angle on some information that allows audiences to consume it more readily. If you are one of these speakers, then please know that: (a) you are not alone and (b) you can make it big in this industry.

The bottom line here is that you need to be clear on the value you are bringing to the market and you need to know your motivation for getting into this field. Whether you are an inspirational, motivational or topical speaker you'll need to:

- be congruent with your message (you'll read more on this later);

- deliver value to your clients; and,

- most importantly, do something that gives you a sense of purpose and makes you happy.

2.0 TOPICS

Rarely do I send a speaker down the path of straight-up motivation or inspiration these days. Clients want to see a Return on their Investment. So, we go for the outcomes of the work first when developing the marketing, and then sprinkle in the motivation after the fact. It's not that often that someone builds an entire career on motivation or inspiration anymore.

Speaking Versus Training

For the purpose of this book, the information presented mainly deals with keynote speaking. Many keynote speakers have training programs, workshops, consulting, and seminars in their product line, but there are speakers who deliver only keynote speeches. Much of my experience is with keynoting, although the first speaker I represented had a training background. In the early stages of your career, you might explore the training arena in order to precisely identify your specialty or niche. I have known many speakers who want to transition out of training into full-time keynoting, simply because the training avenue is much more demanding (full days versus 60 minutes).

BUSINESS MODELS

Remember the umbrella (Figure A in Chapter 1)? That is your business model. When you go to the Canadian Association of Professional Speakers (CAPS) or the National Speakers Association (NSA) for the first time, ask people about business models (you may prefer to call them distribution channels), and what works for them. Do your homework and then choose a model. You may change it over time and that's okay. There are few speakers who do business in the exact same way and that is what's great about this industry. Perhaps, you will come from another industry and invent an entirely new business model. *Bravo* — be different, be brave. Some sample business models being used today are outlined below.

- 80% keynotes, 20% product sales (books, CDs, video, online seminars, t-shirts, etc.)
- 25% keynotes, 50% consulting, 25% product sales
- 75% training, 15% webinars, 10% radio show
- 50% consulting, 20% speaking, 30% membership and product sales
- 50% training, 25% coaching, 25% keynotes
- 70% coaching, 10% product sales, 20% public seminars
- 100% product online sales (quit speaking entirely)

Several years ago, Joe Calloway, Vic Osteen (Larry Winget's former business manager) and I put on an Advanced Speakers Forum in Toronto for CAPS. The different philosophies and business styles were apparent right from the beginning of the weekend. Larry and Vic's business style couldn't be more different from Joe's, but they both work. Larry Winget has risen to the top 1% of the industry in terms of revenues using a model which, frankly, the majority of speakers could not get away with. Larry has a canned presentation and does not talk to the client or customize, yet he blows the audience away and gets a ton of referral business. Joe's model is the polar opposite. He's extremely hands-on with the client and will sit through two days of conferences before he gives a speech. Larry and Joe have totally different models but both are successful and, more importantly, they are both in the top 1% of the industry.

When it comes to the information in this book — take what works for you and leave the rest behind.

I have learned that it's easy to get caught in the mentality that there is only one way to manage this business successfully. That's just not true. Therefore, when it comes to the information in this book — take what works for you and leave the rest behind. You may decide that a training or a consulting business is more the direction for you — go for it. Refer back to Coaching Exercise 2, A Day in Your Life Five Years from Now, and allow yourself to design a business and a life that is perfect for you.

2.0 JOE, VIC AND LARRY

Larry Winget went on to become even more famous through his own A&E reality show, *Big Spender*, TV commercials, and his best-selling books. Of all of the people in our industry, he's probably carved out one of the more unique business models and I'd encourage you to carve out your own path as well.

Joe Calloway has also carved out a niche for himself in the corporate world. He's constantly reinventing and it's allowed him to flow through turbulent times in our industry without nearly as much financial turmoil as other speakers. Joe broke away from the "keynote only" model long before other speakers. Companies often ask him to interview their CEO or leadership team on stage, rather than give a keynote, and Joe — who is brilliant at making other people look good — loves this new way of delivering his message. What resulted was clients who were thrilled and a new distribution channel. Now Joe tends to talk to smaller groups about how great companies get better and clients are using him in all kinds of unique ways. Joe believes that in a constantly changing marketplace it's a mistake for speakers to get trapped in a business model that limits how speakers can create value for their clients.

2.0 THE FLOW OF YOUR BUSINESS

The way our business flows is something we can all be strategic about (see Figure D). I've been very clear since starting my company, Speaker Launcher, that reading my book would always be the first step for any client. After they know my philosophy on business, then they can continue on and become a client in one of a number of ways — private coaching, Wealthy U (group coaching), online learning (self-study), etc.

FIGURE D: **Revenue Streams**

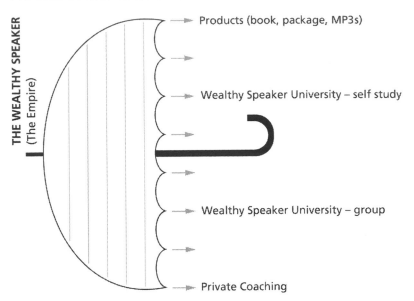

THE WEALTHY SPEAKER
(The Empire)

Products (book, package, MP3s)

Wealthy Speaker University – self study

Wealthy Speaker University – group

Private Coaching

 2.0 ⬤ **Coaches Question:** *How do you want your business to flow? Map out the ideal scenario. Which revenue stream is your rain maker? What does that lead to? It may not always happen as you plan, but the more strategic we are, the more we can control these things.*

⚡ FLASHPOINT: Rick Butts

On September 11, 2001, like a lot of speakers, I was stuck in a galaxy far, far from home — Phoenix, AZ. I wasn't about to drive a rental car back to Denver — and as the next three days unfolded I watched as speeches canceled or "postponed" — and my income went down the tubes.

I decided right then that I would never again be dependent upon the travel industry — or anyone else if I could help it — to make a good income. Starting another business that was non-linear — meaning I wasn't the product — was my goal, vision, and dream.

I found a small group of people selling downloadable information products on the Internet and attended a conference in

Las Vegas to learn about this model. This was the ideal business for me — and for any speaker with subject knowledge.

Many of my speaking skills translated into cyber-applications like mini-courses, tele-seminars, audio and video products, consulting and pdf downloads. You see, it was just speaking without getting on an airplane!

I set a goal to equal, or surpass, my speaking income with my part-time Internet business income. When that day came two years later, I was scared to death to walk away from the big speaking paychecks. But, I made the move and have never regretted it. Online marketing has changed my life in a beautiful way. Eleven years of speaking and traveling fulfilled that dream — now I am helping people all over the world, using all my skills and learning new things every day. And I don't miss my beaten up roller bag, airport security lines, delayed flights, or 1 a.m. arrivals at mediocre hotels.

Rick's story shows us all that we should be thinking about building a business model that works for us. In this next story, Bob Parker has learned that collaboration and uniqueness can be the key to building a successful long-term business model. His career soared once he developed his Pit Crew Challenge brand. Bob (and colleagues) deliver leadership and team-building programs designed around a race car experience. He's had tremendous success and works all over the world.

2.0 FLASHPOINT: Bob Parker

Hindsight being what it is, if I had to do it all over again, I'd start in the middle of my speaking career ... it would have been that much easier.

The start of my speaking career began with a passion for speaking and then I developed my expertise along the way. I was young and naïve about this business; I now know I would have had much greater success earlier if I had started from my expertise and developed the speaking skill along the way. I learned that clients don't hire speakers, they hire people who can solve problems — speaking is one means to that end.

I did persevere and once I established my expertise with my clients, the rest came much more easily. This meant deciding what I do speak about and what I don't — "picking-a-lane," and appreciating that others in this business have their lane, but we can all share the road. Very early in my career I understood that I have colleagues and not competitors, and this opened the door for mentoring, coaching, and learning so I could develop that expertise that helped me grow in my business. Some days I got the business, other days my colleagues landed it; this helped me understand the importance of collaboration for larger projects and continued growth in the business.

Those who want it all for themselves are not big thinkers, they are actually small-minded, as they lose sight of greater opportunities for growth and development in this business. When I'm onstage or in front of an audience, I might be there by myself, but never feel like I'm "going-it-alone," as nothing in my opinion could be more frightening. Having someone who can give you support, feedback, opportunities for growth, and affirmations are all critical to developing skill and success in any endeavor — including speaking.

MAKING MONEY IN YOUR JAMMIES

Our industry has changed over the past few years. It used to be that speakers earned their income one speech, one training session or one consulting gig at a time. That is no longer the case. Many of our colleagues are earning tens of thousands of dollars each month by sharing their knowledge through mediums other than speaking — Rick Butts' Flashpoint story is a great example. In some cases, this includes product sales and information marketing via the Internet.

Do your due diligence to make sure that speaking is what you want to be doing on a daily basis. Many speakers have decided to put the keynotes aside and strictly market their knowledge through technology. We lovingly call this the "make money in your jammies" club. That is what's perfect for them. And please note that in order to be successful, you have to know

You need to learn about information marketing.

what you are doing — the people making the most money spend hours and hours developing systems that involve a ton of technology. Many people are in the game; few are getting rich.

Go back to Coaching Exercise 2, A Day in Your Life Five Years from Now, and think about how you want to spend your day and continue to build the vision. Know that as you get more and more familiar with information marketing, this might change. I'd suggest building the business in phases, so that you don't become overwhelmed with every-thing there is to do. Which phase comes first will be based on where your passion lies. If platform speaking is your first priority, you might consider leaving the information marketing until phase III, but don't try to learn it all at once or you will suffer information overload.

Crunch the Numbers

I heard a second-hand story of a speaker meeting with her accoun-tant to review her product and online marketing initiatives for the past several years. She had invested thousands of dollars in new product and online marketing ideas that had netted her very little. Her accountant suggested that had she simply put that money into a retirement fund, 401K or RRSP, she would have had $1 million extra for retirement. Think long and hard and crunch the numbers on your initiatives before taking the leap into a product line or information marketing operation. You may be bet-ter simply investing your profits, than trying to hit the jackpot in the information marketing game. The experts make it look easy to earn millions each year, but they spend enormous amounts of time studying and honing their operations.

WEBSITE REFERENCE TOOL

www.speakerlauncher.com ➡
Book Buyer LOGIN *(red button)*

For more on information marketing, check out the work of Tom Antion, Bob Scheinfeld, and Randy Gage.

You may be better simply investing your profits, than trying to hit the jackpot in the information marketing game.

Taking Action

We were on a flight back from Phoenix and Kevin (who's name I changed to protect the lazy) was complaining to me that he hadn't learned anything at the NSA convention. He told me he had attended several speaker events in the past 18 months and really wasn't excited. When I probed a little further, it turned out he hadn't applied anything he had learned — all of the knowledge he had been gathering was sitting at home in a drawer. Kevin and I made a pact just as the plane was landing. He was going to do two things differently in the next year.

1. He was going to start taking action on all of the things he had learned in the past 18 months; and

2. He wasn't going to attend any more learning events until he had completed #1.

Whether you are a speaker who is just launching your career or someone who has been in the industry for years, my goal is for you to get many juicy ideas from this book. More importantly, *I want you to take action!* Whether it be changing the way you introduce yourself or an overhaul of your entire marketing program — action is the key.

Ready, Aim, Fire

Have you ever put together a marketing campaign or designed a new one sheet or promotional piece that was a total flop? I have. Have you ever blown several hundred, or several thousand, dollars on an idea that just didn't work? I have.

Our industry is full of ideas. Does this scenario sound familiar? You go to a speaker convention or workshop and you get an idea that inspires you. You come home and give it a try. It flops.

So what's the problem? You're hitting *fire* before you get *ready* and take *aim*. You have to stop and ask yourself a few questions before taking ideas and putting them into action. You have to see whether or not this idea fits with your business model and what you are trying to accomplish.

I just hung up the phone from a coaching client, Jake, who is a serial-firer. Jake was unclear of his message and his target market, yet he had been calling companies already to try to book speaking engagements. He told me he had tried several marketing ideas that had failed. The reason? You guessed it: fire, ready, aim. There was no rhyme or reason to the ideas — Jake was shooting randomly.

We started at the beginning and began to build a foundation for Jake's business. What was his key message? What were the benefits to the audience? Who was his target market? What marketing materials would he need to reach them? Etc. Once this strategy was in place, Jake had a much stronger foundation from which to start.

Keep the Idea Barometer (see Figure E) handy and before you put any idea to the test, ask yourself the seven pertinent questions.

FIGURE E: **Idea Barometer**

Test your ideas on the barometer before you put them into action.

1. Can I afford this idea?	
2. Does it fit with my overall business strategy?	
3. Does it fit with my vision of my business?	
4. Can I implement this idea successfully?	
5. Will this idea get me closer to my goal?	

| 6. What is the payoff? | |
| 7. Do I know of several people who have implemented this idea with good results? | |

Those are just a few basic questions for evaluating your existing ideas as well as the ones in this book. From here on, I'm going to walk you through much of the process so you won't be shooting randomly any more.

2.0 READY, AIM, FIRE

Let me share with you a few of my flops that resulted due to lack of a strategy, lack of Ready, Aim, Fire.

The Wealthy Speaker going into bookstores was one. My market is reasonably small and specialized — about 20,000 people. I can't attribute that much revenue or credibility is derived from being in the bookstores for this product. Of course, it was difficult to know this until I had hit "fire." The money I lost simply from lowering the price of the book to the brutal rate that bookstores require was huge. And the way bookstores handle returns and the number of middle-men in the book chain is "redonculous!" It's a very dysfunctional industry, which is why writers like Seth Godin took matters into their own hands and swore off traditional publishing.

So, if you're writing a book, really consider your distribution strat-egy. If you're in a small market, like mine, then perhaps you stick to working through Amazon, your own website, and some specialty markets. The key for you is going to be speaking audiences — those may become your primary distribution channel. Imagine pre-selling 500 books to one audience. That's so much easier than slogging away one bookstore sale at a time!!!

Another mistake I made was with my second book. (A total depar-ture from *The Wealthy Speaker* — those of you who follow me on Twitter or Facebook know this story well.) *The Frog Whisperer* was born from my private struggle to find love in my life. When I put a strategy into place, I finally met and married my prince (I use that term loosely ☺). Anyway, my mistake with *The Frog Whisperer* was launching the book without a solid following. Please learn from this mistake!

Had I been smarter, I would have started blogging and writing in the field of love and dating for three years before launching the book. That way, like in my speaking business, I would have had a solid following who were waiting to receive the book. The Frog book is a much better fit for the bookstores since it's more of a mass appeal, but the bookstores don't know me or my platform in this genre so it's a difficult sell. (For more on this other side of my life go to *www.frogwhisperer.com*.) Since I had no intention of speaking on this topic, in hindsight, I think I would have passed on the project all together. This also goes back to my lesson about staying in "your lane" — see Picking a Lane in Phase I: Ready for more on this.

The Wealthy Speaker University was another lesson. At first I started to put together an event for speakers. Two days where we'd all come together and share ideas. I went down the road, booked the hotel and put together the marketing for this event when I realized that this isn't what I want to be selling. First, there are now tons of events for speakers to choose from each year. Then I realized that what I do best is better accomplished over a period of time, so people can get the work done and then come back to me for more. So I scrapped the entire weekend event and started over. I came back to my market with what is now known as The Wealthy Speaker University which is now a 12-month group learning program and a big success.

Sales Sidebar

Now why do I tell you about these types of projects that I have on the go? Two reasons.

1. I want you to get ideas for your business, for you to be thinking, "Hey, what's my version of the University?"

2. I'm doing what you all should be doing when you write books or blog posts — planting seeds. I want you to know everything that is going on in my world so that you'll want to buy it! (Not just a pretty face here people!)

2.0 *Coaches Question: When you're setting out to develop a new idea, ask yourself, "What is my intention here?" When you have that clear, then follow Ready, Aim, Fire.*

Phases of the Wealthy Speaker Process

Figure F outlines the steps that we'll take walking through the Ready, Aim, Fire process. No matter how far along you are in your career, it's never too late to go back to the beginning and ensure that you are on the right track — especially if you are not getting all of the business you want. In the case of an experienced speaker, you'll probably be getting more focused. In the case of the beginning speaker, we'll go step by step through the phases so that you are crystal clear on what you bring to the market before you start firing out marketing programs.

When you are clear on your intentions for your speaking business, follow Ready, Aim, Fire.

FIGURE F: **The Wealthy Speaker Process**

Phase	Action	
PHASE I: **READY**	Focus	What am I selling? What is my expertise? Who is going to buy this? How will I position this and create a brand?
PHASE II: **AIM**	Marketing	Update or design marketing materials that reflect your positioning and brand. How do I best explain what this is and the benefits?
PHASE III: **FIRE**	Roll Out	Who is my target market and how will I reach them? What consistent actions do I need to take to build momentum?

Now I'd like you to take a little pledge to ensure that you will follow the steps presented in this book — so that you can avoid firing out of sequence.

THE PLEDGE:

I _____ (state your name) will no
longer FIRE marketing ideas or any idea at random.
I will focus and get READY and check my market
before taking AIM and finally FIRE. I will ask myself
all seven pertinent questions before I FIRE.

_____

Signed

Action Steps
• •

In each phase of the Wealthy Speaker Process, there will be action
steps — tasks that must be completed in order for you to move forward and start building momentum. For example, in Phase I: Ready,
where you are focusing on what you are selling, an action item might
be to take your speech idea to a few of your colleagues or prospective
clients to see if they would buy it. Or join Toastmasters so that you
have a place to practice new speech material. Don't allow the "to dos"
that pop into your head as you are reading distract you from the process. Put them on your list, so that you can continue to move forward.
If you find yourself feeling reluctant about completing these tasks,
take a look at the following coach's question and read Ron's Story.
Just make sure that fear — or your gremlin — isn't driving the bus.

COACH'S QUESTION: *What will I allow to get in my way of
starting this business?*
    *Really examine anything that you might allow to get in your
way. Is it based on fear? Or is it legit? If it's something like your
child's illness, you'll obviously need to pay attention and give
yourself a break for allowing the process to be derailed. But don't
allow distractions, confusion, lack of time or lack of knowledge
stop you. You can work through every one of those situations if*

you are dedicated to this goal. When you find yourself spinning your wheels, you can usually stop to see that self-sabotage — your gremlin — is at work somewhere below the surface.

Now turn to the Action Steps Form in Coaching Exercise 3. It is the "to do" list of things that you don't want to forget.

RON'S STORY

Ron was a successful corporate man. He had climbed to VP of several Fortune 500 companies and was launching his speaking business. Every week Ron and I would have our coaching call and Ron would give me a list of reasons explaining why he hadn't accomplished anything. I allowed this to go on for three consecutive weeks. Then I posed the big question: "What's stopping you from moving forward in your speaking career." When Ron took an honest look at the situation, he realized that he was sabotaging himself. Why?

He was afraid of stepping into something so foreign to him. He was used to being the guy with the solid reputation, the one that his company could count on, the golden boy. Now, no one would know him, he had to start over to build a reputation and that, understandably, was scary. How this affected Ron was that he couldn't or wouldn't take any of the actions necessary to get started until he addressed the fear. Ron was letting his gremlin drive the bus.

2.0 ACTION STEPS

Many people use different "Apps" or tools to help them move through projects. I have high-tech and low-tech apps. My high-tech app is called Evernote and it sits on my laptop, in my iPad and on my iPhone. So when I get an idea, I add it to the appropriate note in Evernote and I have it wherever I need it. There are also some great project planning apps — find one that works for you. My low-tech app is a giant Post-It Note Flip Chart (thank you 3M). I take off a page and stick it to my white board and this is where I list the big things on my to do list. Between this and Evernote, nothing important ever falls through the cracks.

Coaching Exercise 3: ACTION STEPS FORM

In each phase of the Wealthy Speaker Process, there will be action steps — tasks that must be completed in order for you to move forward and start building momentum. The Action Item List is the "to do" list of things you don't want to forget.

If you don't own *The Wealthy Speaker Workbook and Planning Guide*, take a copy of this form, or develop your own system, for listing the ideas on which you must act and assigning a timeline to them. If you work best using spreadsheets, then by all means develop a spreadsheet. If you want to start a binder for everything, then do that. Only you know how you work best.

What's important is that you take action in order of priority and with deadlines attached.

"By When" means by what date do you want the action step completed. You may break the book down into segments in order of their importance. For example, your "A" priority might be the speech, your "B" might be developing a brand, "C" might be your website, etc. Each phase will have several action steps. When each segment is complete, you can come back and work on the next segment. You may have a separate form for each segment.

ACTION ITEM LIST		
Action Step	Priority	By When

ACTION ITEM LIST		
Action Step	Priority	By When

You can also find all of these exercises in a separate and conveniently bound workbook: *Wealthy Speaker Workbook and Planning Guide.*

2.0 THE VALUE OF COACHING

I just got off the phone with Allison, one of my top coaching clients. She's very self-aware and realized years ago that when it comes to website copy, she can totally get derailed. In the past, the task of developing the copy would have put her on hold for several months and even then she would struggle to get it complete. This year, she hired a coach (me) to keep her moving forward. We blew through her web copy problem in 30 minutes rather than 3 months. So is there some value in having a coach on your team? You tell me.

This story may sound self-promotional, if so, okay! I want you to be thinking about your weak links and who might be on your team to support you past them. If that's me, then great.

Sales Sidebar

This is me asking for the business, sales 101. Are you asking for the business in your books?

The Basics: Setting Up a Speaker's Office
• •

The speaking business, like any other business, requires some preparation and set up. The checklist in Coaching Exercise 4 will help guide you through the necessary steps. You can begin building these items into your Action Item List (Coaching Exercise 3) based on the urgency of each item. By physically setting up a business, you are announcing to yourself and to the world that, "I'm now ready and open for business!"

Here's a description of things you will need to get your business off the ground. Use the checklist in Coaching Exercise 4, but refer back to these explanations as you move through the process.

SPEECH

If you're speech is not ready for market, then you need to spend some time on this before setting up. No point in opening a candy store when you don't have the candy, right? Your speech is the most important part of this equation. Seek help through books, tapes, coaching, Toastmasters, NSA, wherever you can to get this component in place. We'll discuss how to know if your speech is good enough in Chapter 3.

BRANDING

Branding yourself, your speech or your business will take some creative thought. You will want to develop a company name and logo. The completion of this task will lead you to the physical representations — the business cards, letterhead, etc. Finally you'll need a website and URL. You may want to enlist the help of marketing and/ or design professionals.

2.0 BRANDING

A huge part of building a brand today revolves around social media. So add to your list the following:

- Facebook Business Page,
- LinkedIn Account,
- Twitter Account and
- Blog (this will be an add-on to your website in most cases).

We'll get into more details on these in Phase II: Aim. But if you get the basics in place at the beginning, you can start to build a following right away.

I've placed what I deem the "holy trinity" of social media here — okay, so there are four, but you get the idea — but even at this date Google+ and Pinterest are picking up major steam. Your goal is to assess the new platforms and decide whether or not to jump in!

OFFICE SET-UP

This is the nuts and bolts of your business.

Dedicated Phone Line — You are not "in" business if you are sharing the phone line with your home phone. I'd recommend not getting call waiting on your business line — it doesn't look professional when you ask a client to hold. Let the calls roll over into voice mail. Also, you'll want to have the phone company's voice mail system and not an answering machine. It's more professional.

Look at all of the "traditional" things required to run a business and ask yourself, "Do I really need this?"

Fax Machine and Dedicated Fax Line — Many phone companies offer you a fax line with distinctive ring so that you don't have to pay for another line. It's a good option but don't have a distinctive ring on your main business line or you will miss faxes while doing business. You might combine your personal and distinctive ring lines, but only if you don't have a busy personal line. People with teenagers better have a dedicated line for each. Think it all through. It might be easier to get separate lines right from the beginning.

Mailing Station — This doesn't need to be fancy. A simple card table can serve as a place to pack up product and marketing materials to go out the door. Design everything as a system so that everything is at your finger-tips.

EQUIPMENT

Some of the equipment you'll need is common to setting up any business, but speakers need a few specialized items.

Computer — I am of the opinion that it is extremely hard to set up a speaker's office, or any business, without computer skills. Get a quality machine and make sure you back up your data frequently. If you need training, it should be at the top of your Action Item List.

Accounting System Software — Consult with an accountant to set up your books so you get it right from the beginning of your business. Make sure you set up your office expenses, which can include some of your home expenses too. See more on this in Chapter 7 under The High-Tech Speaker on the Road.

File Drawers/File Folders — You might consider color-coding your files for easy access: Administration, Marketing, Product Development (speeches, books, etc.), Clients. Your personal files should be a separate color too.

Calendar — The giant 12-month kind with space to write in each day is best. You'll want to switch to an electronic calendar like eSpeakers eventually, but this is a good visual starting place. I used to use round dots — green for booked events and yellow for light holds. I'd write the client name and city inside the dot. See more on this in Chapter 7 under The High-Tech Speaker on the Road.

> **WEBSITE REFERENCE TOOL**
>
> www.speakerlauncher.com ➡
> Book Buyer LOGIN *(red button)*
> **Check out:** eSpeakers for more information on accounting system software and electronic calendars.

ADMINISTRATION

These tasks involve an outside agency.

Business License — Find out if you need one and then follow all the required regulations.

Tax Number — Again, you might not need this until you reach a certain income level.

Business Bank Accounts — You'll want your banker on your side right from the beginning. You may consider setting up a line of credit. If you plan on working in the U S and Canada, you may consider accounts in both currencies, but wait until you have the need unless the accounts do not charge service fees.

 ## CHECKLIST

Really take a look at all of the "traditional" things required to run a business and ask yourself, "Do I really need this?" Perhaps you won't ever need a piece of formal letterhead? Perhaps you don't need to establish a second land line for your phone — maybe a Skype phone number would suffice? Do people really send faxes anymore? That might be one you can do away with too. This is your business. Set it up based on what's current. When I was setting up my Frog business, I needed a Shopping Cart and Merchant Account (for product sales) and some letterhead to place with the orders, return labels, etc. But I didn't need a fax machine for that business and there was very little paperwork that wasn't virtual so I didn't need a file drawer.

WEBSITE REFERENCE TOOL

www.speakerlauncher.com ➡
Book Buyer LOGIN *(red button)*

Recommended Reading: *Business for Beginners* by Frances McGuckin — everything regarding your office and business set up.

Coaching Exercise 4: CHECKLIST FOR SETTING UP A SPEAKER'S OFFICE

Here's a checklist of things you will need to get your business off the ground. Refer back to the explanations in the text if you need more direction.

___ **Speech**

___ **Branding**

    ___ Company Name/Logo

    ___ URL — name for website

    ___ Business Cards

    ___ Letterhead

    ___ Return Labels

___ **Branding 2.0**

    ___ Facebook Business Page

    ___ LinkedIn Account

    ___ Twitter Account

    ___ Blog

___ **Office Set-Up**

    ___ Dedicated Phone Line

    ___ Fax Machine and Dedicated Fax Line

    ___ Mailing Station

___ Equipment

    ___ Computer

    ___ Accounting System Software

    ___ File Drawers/File Folders

    ___ Calendar

___ **Administration**

    ___ Business License

    ___ Tax Number

    ___ Business Bank Accounts

You can also find all of these exercises in a separate and conveniently bound workbook: *Wealthy Speaker Workbook and Planning Guide.*

Phase I

READY

Focus on Positioning
and the Speech

· ·

Phase I of the Wealthy Speaker Process enables the speaker to focus
on getting ready for this new career. You must focus on which topic
area will bring you the most success — that will get you to your
picture of A Day in Your Life Five Years from Now (see Coaching
Exercise 2). Then you'll take this decision a step further and focus
on becoming a true expert in this area and position yourself as the
expert. Finally, developing a killer speech is the final stage on which
to focus at this phase. As in many life tasks, preparation is key and
focusing on this "get ready" phase is vital in the process.

The Wealthy Speaker Gets Ready
· ·

Imagine you are a meeting planner (someone who hires speakers)
and you are looking for a speaker to talk about leadership. You start
looking online and you find four speakers who do leadership plus

several other topics. Then someone recommends a speaker who wrote the book on leadership and delivers only that topic. Who would you pick? The jack of all trades or the master of one?

Who would you pick? The jack of all trades or the master of one?

• • • • • • • • • • • •

Of course you want the best for your group, the expert, the guru. As a speaker it is possible to offer services on a few related topics and perform well. But as a Wealthy Speaker, you want to be the expert — the one meeting planners call upon for a speech on that topic. So you need to focus your attention and talents on one topic area. My friend Joe Calloway calls this "picking a lane."

PICK A LANE

One of my clients, Greg Schinkel, had been building a training company for over ten years. They did corporate training on several topics and he was hired to do the occasional keynote. Greg came to me with the goal to expand his keynote speaking business. The obstacle was that Greg had not become known in the industry for any one thing. His company had become the jack of all trades and the master of none — they provided training on managerial skills, sales, customer service, time management, etc. After crunching the numbers, Greg decided to drop many of his less profitable training courses and focus solely on what he did best, leadership. He had already written a book on leadership and had the expertise to back it up.

Almost immediately Greg's business shifted and he started doing more leadership consulting, which then resulted in keynotes and training on that topic. Greg's profits also rose. He was no longer trying to please everyone and it was a huge relief. He trimmed his staff, offering his people contract work instead of full-time employment and he moved his office to a less expensive location, cutting his overhead in half. Even Greg's health improved as the stress of running the training company was alleviated. In the first year, they were more profitable than in the entire ten year history of the company. The minute Greg stopped spinning his wheels trying to please everyone and focused his time, energy and resources on one area of expertise, business started to flood in the door.

This entire book is filled with success stories about my clients. You should be filling your books with good-news stories and case studies about the various offerings you have. If you coach, tell stories about coaching clients; if you keynote, tell stories about keynotes. This plants seeds in the minds of your readers for future business.

2.0 GREG SCHINKEL UPDATE

What a difference a few years can make when you are on the right track! In 2004, my training business was basically insolvent. I was generating sales but no profits. Instead of a growing bank account, I was accumulating more debt.

I made two big changes — I left behind many of the "I can do that" topics that littered my marketing and promo and reduced my overhead so that I could be profitable in good times and bad.

Since Jane's help with making these two changes my sales revenues have doubled, my expenses have been reduced, and my net income and cash flow have increased by ten times. My only regret is that it took me 13 years to figure this out. Picking my lane helped my Internet inquiries jump to the point where most new business comes from Google search, referrals, or past clients.

Stop spinning your wheels. Focus your time, energy and resources on one area of expertise. Business will flood in the door.

My lifestyle is getting closer to the one envisioned during my coaching with Jane. I'm still working more hours than I ultimately want to, but I'm enjoying the fruits of my labor.

CHANGING LANES

A more experienced speaker — even an expert — may find a change is needed. Maybe the 500th delivery of the same speech becomes unsatisfying or perhaps your career has leveled out. Whatever the circumstance, it is important to focus on the new topic — signal and change lanes. Or perhaps you just need to tweak your existing lane to breathe new energy into it. Changing lanes is scary. There's no question. It takes huge courage, but the future of your business probably depends on it.

My buddy, Joe Calloway, posed a question to the audience at the NSA National Convention in Phoenix in July 2004 that still has relevance: "What do you need to let go of in order to take your business to the next level?"

What Joe didn't tell the audience was the story of how he threw out all of his speech materials and started from scratch in order to move to a new and better place in his career. Most speakers would die if they had to throw away their speech. But it worked for Joe — big time. He had been a motivational speaker (and a damn good one) for more than ten years. All the bureaus loved him and booked him like crazy because he delivered one of the best speeches in the business. But Joe wasn't satisfied. His fees and his career had reached a plateau. He needed a new challenge.

Joe had been moving in the direction of business for awhile and he boldly decided to toss his entire motivational speech. He started from scratch as a business expert and he eventually moved into the more specific area of branding. Joe was approached by a reputable publishing house (John Wiley & Sons) to write a book and *Becoming a Category of One* positioned him beautifully as the expert in this field. The risk paid off. Joe started working with companies at the CEO and senior executive level and he felt his work was the best of his career. He had reinvented himself and his fees and demand went through the roof.

Sometimes moving to a new level means being brave. Don't get stuck doing things you are "good at."

I see a direct correlation between plugging into your true passion or purpose and how much income you earn. The more passion — the more revenue. If you are a speaker who has been "phoning in" your speech for any length of time, you are due for a change. Sometimes moving to a new level means being brave. Don't get stuck doing things you are "good at." I challenge you to see where your path takes you next.

So how do you pick a lane or change lanes? The Focus Form in Coaching Exercise 5 will help you pick a lane.

Coaching Exercise 5: FOCUS FORM

A good speaker can talk on a variety of topics, but a Wealthy Speaker focuses on one topic, one expertise, one set of speech materials — or even one speech — under the same umbrella. If you want to be the recognized expert — the one that meeting planners call upon when they need a speaker on that topic — you need to bring all your skill and energy to that topic. You must pick a lane.

Review the sample below and follow the process to complete the Focus Form.

Sample _____

Joan is a former real estate broker who loves helping women take control of their lives. She has proven it over and over in her own life and business, and she's thought about writing a book on the topic. Joan also breeds champion quarter horses and has been asked to speak several times on that topic. And as an experienced real estate broker, she's been speaking and training for years.

Joan would like to launch a speaking career. She needs to consider what she wants to be doing in her speaking business five years from now and where her passion and purpose lie.

Notice the scores she gives herself on the Take Control of Your Life speech. This speech, if she works hard on the delivery, could be the one for which she becomes known and gets paid (well) to deliver. The higher the demand, the higher her fees can go. The more enthusiastic she is about the topic and the more purposeful it feels to her, then the more contagious a response she will have in her audiences, creating more demand. Women will tell other women, "You have to hear this message!"

FOCUS FORM: **Sample**

Area of Expertise	Passion/Purpose	Revenue	Vision	Credibility	Relevance	Uniqueness	Talent	TOTAL
Sales: How to Sell More Real Estate	5	8	8	7	8	6	7	49
Breeding Champion Quarter Horses	8	4	6	7	7	8	7	47
Take Control of Your Life — for Women	9	8	9	9	8	8	8	59

STEP 1: Review the example to understand the process.

STEP 2: List all of your speech ideas (things you could talk about) down the left-hand side.

STEP 3: Rate each of your speeches on a scale of 1 to 10 — 10 being a perfect fit with the criteria listed across the top.

Here are some questions to ask yourself when rating the criteria below:

> *Passion:* How passionate am I about this project? Is it in line with what I'm meant to do in this world?
>
> *Revenue:* Is it a high revenue generator (8) or low (2)? Who will pay to hear this message? (This one is key!)
>
> *Vision:* Does it fit with my long-term business vision? Can I see myself loving this topic in five years? Is it an area into which I want to immerse myself?
>
> *Credibility:* Does it fit with my background and credibility? Am I walking my talk of this topic?
>
> *Relevance:* Is the message timely and relevant for the audience?
>
> *Uniqueness:* Is my message or delivery unique?
>
> *Talent:* Am I really great at this?

STEP 4: Add the totals across and you should see which speech makes the most sense to proceed with. This is your lane!

FOCUS FORM

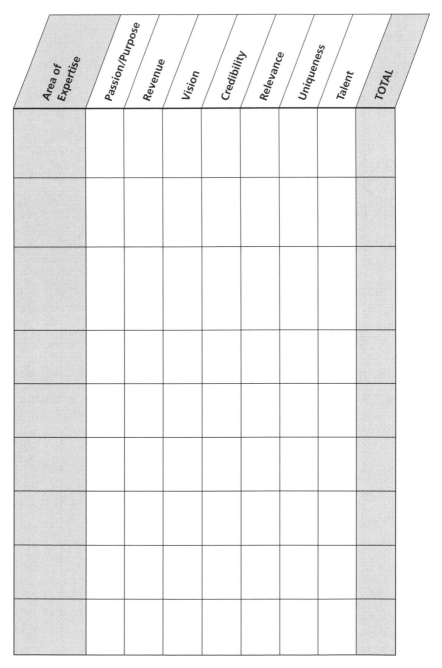

Area of Expertise	Passion/Purpose	Revenue	Vision	Credibility	Relevance	Uniqueness	Talent	TOTAL

You can also find all of these exercises in a separate and conveniently bound workbook: *Wealthy Speaker Workbook and Planning Guide.*

THE COSMIC 2 X 4

It happens all the time. We nestle into a job, a speech or a business model and we allow complacency to wash over us like a warm bubble bath. It's comfortable. But then the universe (or your belief system or your subconscious) kicks in and decides to give you a sign that you need a change. First, it's a small sign and you feel a tad discontented. Then bigger signs start to appear. And then, if you still aren't taking notice, you receive a cosmic two-by-four across the back of the head. What does this feel like? You get fired from a job. You lose your biggest training client. You burn out and get sick. Don't wait until the two-by-four hits before you make a move.

I was working with Vince Poscente and we were moving into our fifth year together. I had achieved all of my goals with Vince, but I loved working with him. We had built the business from ten speeches per year at $2,500 each to 80 speeches per year at $10,000. We had developed a strong product line and our bureau relationships were solid. I could easily have sat on my laurels and put the money in the bank. But things started to go wrong.

First, it was small things — handouts didn't arrive at an event on time. Then the signs started to get bigger and bigger. The cosmic two-by-four came when a scheduling error had caused Vince to miss an engagement. I felt horrible — he had never missed a gig. It was a small freebie engagement as a favor to one of Vince's friends, but that didn't matter. It was a very big sign that something needed to change. I could do the job with my eyes closed — and I needed a wake up call.

I remember feeling so devastated about leaving Vince, but the time had come for me to move on. A week later, Vince's wife Michelle — who ran the speakers' bureau with whom we shared office space — came to me with the idea that I should work for her. The funny thing is that I had the idea at the exact same time. Moving over to the bureau was an easy transition since the two companies had always been close. I had helped the bureau agents over the years and they had helped me learn how to book Vince. It was the best move I could have made and I thank the universe for giving me that whack on the side of the head.

It's easy to get stuck at something at which you excel, but if you stay stuck, that cosmic two-by-four is inevitable. It is better to let go before it hits. Use the points listed below to help let go.

- Learn to recognize signs that it's time for a change.
- Allow yourself time to consider your options and ask "What's next for me?"
- Look at change as an opportunity for growth rather than something to fear.
- Figure out what you need to "let go of" in order to crank it up a notch. Is it a speech that you've been giving for so long that you're bored? Training that's been keeping you "busy" for years but makes you no money?
- Don't allow fear to dictate your decisions. Who's driving the bus? You or the gremlin on your shoulder?
- Take the cue from great entertainers like Johnny Carson and Oprah who knew exactly the right time to leave the stage. Don't overstay your welcome.

Positioning: Expert First, Speaker Second

Becoming an expert isn't a requirement for the speaking industry only, it's a requirement to make a living in today's global economy. We must be an expert in order to compete — period. In Thomas Friedman's book, *The World Is Flat*, he talks about how globalization has leveled the playing field for all countries to compete for our jobs. Specializing is the only way to excel in this fast-paced, high-tech world.

We must be an expert in order to compete — period.

⚡ FLASHPOINT: Patricia Fripp, CSP, CPAE

I have been speaking professionally for 25 years and the industry has been extremely kind to me. I've always been busy. In the early 90s, I was being asked to hold multiple dates up to a year in advance and clients were telling me, "We just want you. We'll decide on the topic later." They were buying Patricia Fripp.

Today, people are buying my expertise and it has nothing to do with me. The day that it all changed was when I was speaking to a sales team. The National Sales Manager came up to me after the event and said, "Patricia, I really liked your speech, but more so, I loved the way that you delivered it. Can you teach our sales people to do that?" Her sales team would spend months each year preparing for a presentation that would either close or lose a nine-million-dollar contract for them. Due to poor presentation skills they weren't closing the business.

So I helped them and when word got out, more sales teams came to me for presentation skills and everything changed. My business was always busy, but now it had exploded. I marketed much less and concentrated my efforts on building a great website and generating traffic. I now get a large percentage of my business as a result of the Internet.

If you are making a decision either to market yourself or to market your expertise, I'd go with expertise since it has changed my business so dramatically and earned me more revenue than ever before.

2.0 PATRICIA FRIPP

What has changed is the importance of a web presence, now more than ever. Like many seasoned speakers what keeps me profitable is a balanced business — more virtual aspects to my relationship building and training. A good portion of my business is local, which results from the focused attention towards that goal. Am I making three times more? No. But I am having good steady growth even in a down market.

And I'm more balanced now. For the most part I have retired from NSA chapters. After more than 300 chapter visits since 1984 I want my weekends to myself.

And she deserves her weekends, I've not seen many people who work harder than Patricia Fripp in our industry and I congratulate her on growth in a down market.

2.0 PICKING A LANE

Since writing this book, the idea of picking a lane has become clearer for me. And as with most ideas, there are exceptions to the rule. Last year I started to seek out people who I would consider to be true entrepreneurs. I wanted to study how someone would straddle more than one lane since I was about to embark on this when I introduced my new book, *The Frog Whisperer*. (I had been preaching "pick a lane" for many years, so believe me I was torn about going against my own advice.) Here's what I learned.

My new advice is to have all of your business interests fall under the same umbrella.

Some people have an entrepreneurial spirit and can pull off many different business interests. What my new advice would be is to have all of those business interests fall under the same umbrella. A great example of this is a huge company like Pepsico. They moved into areas like fast foods (Taco Bell, California Pizza Kitchen) and even went as far as transportation (North American Van Lines), but later went back to their core of food and beverage packaged goods.

The role of the entrepreneur is basically one of moving projects forward. You need a team of people in place to help you move all of the ideas forward. It's difficult to do without discipline and focus.

I believe that it is possible to straddle different lanes, but ideally, if you are going to speak to large audiences and build a speaking business, it's much, much easier to become known for one topic area.

POSITION IN THE INDUSTRY

Now that you've picked your lane, you need to focus on how you position yourself as an expert in the industry.

- How are you positioning yourself in the marketplace? As a speaker? Or as an expert?
- When I look at your website, will I see the benefits of you and your expertise?
- When clients are comparing you to your competition, is fee ever a factor? (If it's a huge factor then you are not positioning well enough as an expert.)

- Are you known for one thing? For instance, are you George Smith, the guru of stress management?

- When I read your bio, can I clearly define what makes you a credible expert?

- Is it evident that by hiring you, I'll be getting someone who has vast knowledge in this arena?

Take these positioning questions to heart and really make it clear in your marketing materials in what area you are an expert. In your bio, list a number of things that establish you as an expert and then add that you speak, almost like it's an afterthought.

> **Example:** Along with his bestselling book, *Lower Stress and Be More Productive*, George Smith's stress management and productivity tools have been used throughout corporate America for more than a decade helping executives become more effective. His weekly column "Low Stress Executive" has been running in business publications in over 100 cities for the past seven years. George was voted Entrepreneur of the Year by *Montana Business Magazine* in 2006.
>
> George speaks to more than 10,000 executives each year, teaching them his stress-lowering techniques. One of the leading experts in his field, George's audiences include IBM, Sun Microsystems, Bank One, AT&T and National Association of Business Owners.

Does this make sense? We take all of what makes George an expert and put it up front in the bio, leaving the fact that he is in demand as a speaker until the end. Expert first — speaker second. Now when George is competing for a speaking job, he is the established expert and the fee becomes less of an issue. Clients will probably be familiar with his work and when the need for his topic arises, he becomes the only choice. He has moved from being a commodity as a speaker to an expert who commands the fee of his choosing.

> *A Note About George's Topic*: While you might cover a topic that is always in demand, you also need to stay on top of the current jargon. For instance, stress manage-

ment might be hot one year and out the next. George might consider re-branding in order to keep it fresh.

Becoming the Legitimate Expert

Stating that you are the expert isn't enough; you have to be the expert.

Now, the question becomes how much work do you need to do in order to have a bio as rich as George's? In his book Outliers, Malcolm Gladwell states that it takes 10,000 hours to develop an expertise. Although that's kind of extreme, I do believe that stating that you are the expert isn't enough; you have to be the expert. Don't forget, if you've worked in a field for 20 years, you've got those 10,000 hours. If you are at the beginning of your speaking career you might consider Coaching Exercise 6.

COACH'S QUESTION: *What have I done over and over in my life and career that may help define my expertise?*
An example: as early as age ten when I delivered newspapers, I had a desire to exceed my customer's expectations.

Coaching Exercise 6: BECOMING THE EXPERT

What do I need to do to establish myself as an expert in my market? Your answer might come in the form of a radio show, column, blog, articles in trade publications, writing your book, developing products and tools, serving in volunteer roles in industry associations, etc. You want to publicly link your name with the topic. This approach will add to your credibility as an expert.

Brainstorm and make your list now.

1. _____

_____

2. _____

_____

3. _____

_____

4. _____

_____

5. _____

_____

6. _____

_____

7. _____

_____

8. _____

_____

You can also find all of these exercises in a separate and conveniently bound workbook: *Wealthy Speaker Workbook and Planning Guide.*

What If You're a Celebrity?

Whether you founded a successful company, wrote a bestselling book, have a national radio or TV show, won an Olympic medal, are an entertainer, actor or politician, meeting planners may want to book you to help fill seats or add caché to their event. In some cases, you might be more recognizable for your accomplishment, or the story around you, than for your name. For instance Laurie Skreslet was the first Canadian man to summit Mount Everest. Kim Phuc is the little girl, in the Pulitzer Prize winning photo, running away from the horror of a napalm attack on her village in Vietnam. Both are successful speakers.

Even though you're probably being hired to put bums in seats, your clients still want to know that you'll do a good job from the plat-form. I would encourage you to work hard at giving a killer speech. Why? Because word gets around with meeting planners. If you give a mediocre speech or are difficult to work with, your longevity in the industry will be much more limited. Why not blow their doors off and have them say, "Wow, I didn't expect Jane Doe celebrity to be such a fabulous speaker!"

Erin Brockovich is a great example of someone who could have just shown up, said a few words, and collected the check. But she didn't. She gave a very compelling speech that inspired a room of 1500 professional women. On the other hand, a famous football player is known by meeting planners, bureau agents and speakers to be the guy that is constantly chasing women. Trying to sleep with your clients or audience members is a huge mistake no matter who you are. People know and they talk, and it will hurt your business in the long run.

Often as a celebrity, you can get away without having a demo video, but providing a prospective client with a sample of your pre-sentation could be helpful. Many celebrities will be hired on name alone, but being able to reassure the client that you are actually a good speaker is a good way to go.

In terms of speech content, I've seen many celebrities make the mistake of trying to be a motivational speaker, using all of the "believe and you can achieve" lingo. But that's not what you're being paid to do. They can hear motivational stuff from any speaker. Use your life story as a backdrop for the lessons you learned along the way and build from there. If you don't tell your personal story, then you are most likely missing the mark. The real trick is to take the lessons you learned and help the audience with their challenges. It's a rare celebrity who takes the time to get to know his or her audience. When you turn your story around and make it about them, you are gold.

I recently saw a famous singer/dancer/movie star speak at a National Speakers convention. He oozed talent and he had quite a personal story to tell, having come back from an accident that nearly killed him. But he got up on stage and started rattling off some motivational phrases. I felt ripped off.

Some of you could get up on the stage and spit nickels and your audience would rave about it, but the meeting planners are really the ones you need to impress. Not many people in your world are going to tell you the truth or what you need to hear. I'd encourage you to seek honest answers and feedback, rather than listening to your "fans."

The bottom line is that as a celebrity, you have a responsibility to your client and audience to show up present, humble, and with their needs in mind. Check your ego at the door and do more than expected. You'll be rewarded with a long-term, profitable speaking career.

Getting Clear on What You're Selling

You've picked your lane; you've established your expertise; now you need to focus on how to present this package to the marketplace. For some speakers who have been around awhile, this is the missing piece of the puzzle. You might be unclear on the benefits of what you offer and how to position yourself in the marketplace. This may be one reason why speakers' bureaus aren't booking you in the manner you would like — they just don't *get* what you do! So spell it out for bureaus and your clients and ensure it is conveyed on all your marketing materials. Coaching Exercise 7, Presenting Your Expertise to the Marketplace, will help you identify the benefits you bring to the industry and, more specifically, to your clients.

Coaching Exercise 7: PRESENTING YOUR EXPERTISE TO THE MARKETPLACE

You've picked your lane; you've established your expertise; now you need to focus on how to present this package to the marketplace. For some speakers who have been around awhile, this is the missing piece of the puzzle. So spell it out for your clients and ensure it is conveyed on all your marketing materials.

Here are some questions to help you draw out the information:

1. What are the results of my presentations?

    _____

    _____

2. What am I doing for people? Allow yourself to really explore this question to understand the full value of your expertise.

    _____

    _____

3. What groups am I best in front of? Who really needs this message?

    _____

    _____

4. What is most unique about me?

    _____

    _____

5. How am I credible to speak on this topic?

    _____

    _____

6. How do I best deliver my expertise (coaching, keynotes, training)?

    _____

    _____

You can also find all of these exercises in a separate and conveniently bound workbook: *Wealthy Speaker Workbook and Planning Guide.*

Components of a Great Speech

Your speech may already be developed or you may be starting from scratch. Either way, this section will help you design a speech that will knock 'em dead every time.

A great keynote speaker is someone who can keep an audience mesmerized for up to 90 minutes. They might have people go through a series of emotions or take them on a dramatic journey. Some of the best speeches stay in your memory for years. Here's an example:

> *Clients don't want to hire speakers, they want to hire smart people who happen to speak.*
> *— Brian Palmer, National Speakers Bureau*

> Captain Gerry Coffee spoke at my very first NSA convention in Washington, DC. I can recall vividly his story of being captured and being held as a POW in the Vietnam War. He talked about how the prisoners developed a communication style between them. They used Morse Code to tap out messages to each other between the walls. In fact, I can still hear him using his hand to knock on the wood and how that echoed through the microphone. You could have heard a pin drop in that room of 1500 speakers and there was not a dry eye in the house. The fact that I can remember this so clearly nearly 20 years later tells me something.

Your speech is your best marketing tool — so let's get sharpening that tool!

I referred earlier to a speech given by Joe Calloway at NSA in Phoenix in 2004. Joe's style was a factor in his presentation, but what really seemed to resonate with people was one phrase. The words "let it go" have taken on a life of their own throughout NSA and years later people are still making reference to that phrase. It stuck! Your speech is your best marketing tool — so let's get sharpening that tool! Here are a few coaching questions for you:

- What story will you tell in your speech that people will remember ten years from now?
- What will you do that will impact them?

- How will you deliver your message in a unique manner?
- What phrase or common thread will hold your presentation together?
- How will you make it about them and not you?

WHAT MAKES A GREAT SPEECH?

Here are some really basic points. We'll get into more details later with Tips from the Master: Victoria Labalme.

- Speaking is a craft. So "winging it" is not an option. Write out your speech and practice it. Know exactly how long it takes and be prepared to cut some of it when the meeting planner tells you, "We're running behind."
- It should have a beginning, a middle and an end. And the opening and closing stories have to be powerful and solid.
- Use plenty of stories to illustrate your points. Too much teaching and you'll lose your audience.
- Weave your energy throughout your presentation. Be conscious of when you have bursts of high energy and when you are very calm and soothing to the audience. Energetically, it should be a roller coaster journey.
- Try to have the room set for success. This may look different for everyone, so here are a few of my preferences. Avoid dance floors: a huge gap between you and the audience will stunt your energy. Long, narrow rooms are tough: set them up so you are in the middle of the room with the audience huddled around you. Theater style seating is better than round tables, but I have seen many successful speeches in a luncheon format with huge audiences. Just know you have to work a little harder to keep the attention and the energy.
- Try to avoid distractions like food service. Ask the meeting planner to have coffee and dessert on the tables and all plates removed prior to you starting. Have something prepared for every awkward moment that could potentially occur (waiter drops a tray, cell phone rings, fire alarm goes off). Always be prepared.

- Use your voice, pitch, tone, and pacing to take your audience on a journey.

- Have one central message that ties the speech together. Stay focused on your message and your expertise. Avoid rants.

- Avoid rambling. Remove all of the words that are not important in painting a picture for your audience. If it's not essential — don't say it.

- Do your homework to ensure that you know your audience and how your material can be utilized in their lives. Many speakers use a pre-event questionnaire. You should be interviewing the client (and possibly several members of the audience) as part of your research. On top of your regular questions, you'll want to make sure you are asking the client "what would make my presentation a success in your eyes" and "how will you measure success." Check in with them close to the day of your speech as well. If you are speaking to a corporate or association market, then you must have your finger on the pulse of their business or their industry's. If the cover of the *Wall Street Journal* has a story about your client facing huge layoffs on the day of your speech, then you must be prepared. Aside from the business journals and magazines, additional research for the corporate world is available at *hoovers.com*.

- If you use PowerPoint, use it as a visual aid, not a crutch. In a business presentation, the fewer slides the better. An inspirational presentation (someone who has climbed Everest) can be much more riveting with photos that help the audience feel like they are there with you. Two wonderful examples are Jamie Clarke's Everest presentations and DeWitt Jones, a *National Geographic* photographer. Both use photography within PowerPoint in a stunning way to create an experience for the audience. A great book that references PowerPoint is *The Presentation Secrets of Steve Jobs* by Carmine Gallo.

- Allow your passion and enthusiasm for the topic to shine through. If it doesn't, then you may not be speaking on the right topic. Allow your values to guide you on this point and be brave when it comes to making a change.

- Know your best audience size. Some people know that they really shine in front of a huge crowd, while others will do better with smaller audiences. There is a certain talent for reaching people in the far corner of a room of 1500 — you either have that talent or you must learn it. Either way, know where you fit best.

- Arrive at the event early so that you can see what has gone on before your talk. You might get some material that ties in perfectly — and makes you the hero. It might also save you some embarrassment by not telling a story that's already been told.

- Survey the room. Arriving early also gives you a chance to arrange the room to best suit your needs. For example, if you're not sure that the room will be filled and the chairs are set up in theater style, tape off the back rows using masking tape to try to keep the energy as close to you as possible. Arrange the AV to your best advantage and ensure that there aren't huge objects (like AV equipment) between you and your audience. If there is a dance floor between you and the audience, ask for steps at the front of the stage so that you can keep the energy gap to a minimum.

- Use current references. By 2013, it may no longer be timely to talk about Hurricane Katrina, Enron, or 9/11. Push yourself to remain current in all of your stories and references. Stories that worked ten years ago probably need to be changed or, better yet, tossed out. Trust in your ability to come up with new material and if you need help, then seek it out. A little side note: please know that all speakers travel, therefore all speakers have travel stories about airline employees, hotel staff, etc. Try to use examples that the audience has never heard before. Your audiences may see 20 speakers a year which should keep you motivated to be fresh.

- Be relatable. One of my coaching clients is a multi-millionaire who started his business doing every job himself, including cleaning the toilets. He needs to have a mix of toilet stories that balance out his jet-set millionaire stories or the audience will not be able to relate to him. And if they can't relate, then how will they buy into his theories? There's nothing like a story about changing a child's poopy diaper to level the playing field.

- Make it about them! If you are new to this industry, then unfortunately you missed out on one of the best speakers of our era. His name was Art Berg and he passed away long before his time. Art was a quadriplegic who told the story of how he came back from his injuries to live a "beyond full" life and excel at anything to which he put his mind. The theme was "while the difficult takes time, the impossible just takes a little longer." Art and the speaker that I represented at the time, Vince Poscente, were often sharing the platform and their careers were going along at a parallel pace. But something happened and Art's career took off like wildfire. Later that year I asked him, "What had changed, what was he doing differently?" And he said simply, "I made it about them." Sage advice for any speaker. No matter how the story or message is delivered — in Art's case the story of how his accident changed his life — you can always turn it around and make it about the audience, rather than yourself. Sometimes it means changing the language — from "I" to "you" — and sometimes it's asking the audience a powerful question at the end of a story (see Vince Poscente's Flashpoint story next in this chapter). If this is the only tip you take away from this section — take it to heart and make it about them!

- Be yourself. It wouldn't be uncommon for you to come back from a convention, where you saw a speaker that you thought was awesome, and start to take on traits of that speaker. Fast forward ten years down the road and ten or 15 more conventions, you could easily lose yourself in the mix. I think it's great to learn from other people's techniques and to aspire to be like the best, but always try to maintain your individuality and spin things to suit you. I have a client named Albert who is from Guana in northern Africa. Albert didn't own a pair of shoes until he was eight years old. His story is one of incredible courage and is truly inspirational. Albert was told by the Million Dollar Round Table people that his message was not "businessy" enough for them. So Albert wondered if he needed to change his message. But Albert is not, nor will he ever be, a business speaker. Can he draw more parallels from his story to his business audience? You bet.

- Make sure your introduction is solid and sets you up as an expert first and a speaker second. Tell the MC exactly how you would like it to sound. Even though you will be asked for your introduction ahead of time, always carry a spare copy to events in case of emergencies. Work hard on your introduction — you only have one chance to make this first impression, so do everything you can to control it. The introduction is the beginning of your speech, don't leave it to chance.

- Through Line (see Tips from the Masters: Victoria Labalme for a discussion of her Through Line™ concept later in this chapter): Even veteran speakers will often miss this essential piece. A Through Line is a very tight (short) sentence that you offer up to your audience at the beginning of the speech and then continuously sprinkle throughout the speech. At the end you drive the phrase home. Remember Joe's "Let it Go" speech from Phoenix? Well, duh, guess what his Through Line was? Let it go!

  The Through Line should be short and meaningful. It should be a phrase that people want to repeat to each other. If it's empowering then even better. It may be similar to your promise statement (more on this in Phase II: Aim) but it doesn't have to be the same.

WEBSITE REFERENCE TOOL

www.speakerlauncher.com ➡
Book Buyer LOGIN *(red button)*

Recommended Reading: Carmine Gallo's book, *The Presentation Secrets of Steve Jobs.*

FLASHPOINT: Vince Poscente, CSP, CPAE

In business, there is something called the 'S' curve. It is split into three parts. First, the hardest and most arduous part, is the "pay your dues" section. Second is "flashpoint". This is where your business takes off. Third, is the "fine tuning," where slight modifications can make a difference regarding income.

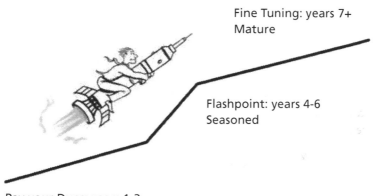

Fine Tuning: years 7+
Mature

Flashpoint: years 4-6
Seasoned

Pay your Dues: years 1-3
New speakers

In the "pay your dues" part of my business I focused on two things: great speaking skills and a preview video that got business. To improve my speaking I just wanted to be at least one percent better in this speech than I was last time. The technique that I used was to use language about my Olympic story, replacing "I" language with "you" language. For example, instead of telling a story about training on top of a car in first person, I used the second person perspective. In the following examples, notice how you feel in the "me" version as opposed to the "you" version.

> "me" Version: I needed to figure out how to get wind tunnel training with a $5 budget. So I found a friend with a really fast car and disturbing disinterest regarding my physical well being.

> "you" Version: Imagine, you needed to figure out how to afford wind tunnel training with only $5 in the budget.

What would any sane person do? You find a friend with a really fast car and a disturbing disinterest for your physical well being.

This one change took several talks to get perfect, but it literally changed how audiences reacted to my presentation. The buzz was building during this "pay your dues" part of my business.

Meanwhile, I was constantly redoing my preview video. My first one didn't bring in a wave of business. Reluctantly, I did another video for meeting planners to book me. Still no luck. Then a third. Still disappointing results. Then the light bulb went off for me. I had to keep redoing preview videos and improving my speaking skills until I hit "flashpoint."

On the seventh preview video in two-and-a-half years the stars aligned. The buzz about my speech (directly due to the use of "you" language) and a killer preview video resulted in about $150,000 in business in six weeks. I hit flashpoint and immediately popped up to around 80 speeches that year.

2.0 VINCE POSCENTE

Having hit the highs of opening keynotes for the National Speakers Association, Million Dollar Round Table (the Carnegie Hall of speaking), plus being inducted into two speaker halls of fame — in Canada and the U.S.A. — I felt on top of the world. Yet, throw in a dash of ego-driven invincibility, best guess brand reinvention (towards Speed) with a long-term recession and I found my keynote business drop 75%.

Overnight I went from pulling in six-figure months to a calendar hoping for a six-figure year. The marketplace had changed and I didn't. At the time of writing this, I continue to look at the vast array of reinvention opportunities. Reinvention is easy to say but, like any start-up, it's about going back to basics. Here's what I've learned about the speaking business today.

- First, the demand for speakers to fill an agenda has flipped to a demand for experts who may or may not be good speakers. *Be an expert!*

- Second, if you want to speak, you must broaden your intellectual property (IP) in a variety of ways like distance learning, coaching, training, consulting, or any other avenue for offering your expertise. *Scale your IP!*

- Third, make sure your brand is easy to comprehend. My brand went from high energy keynotes to "speed" as I mentioned above. But I learned — the expensive way — if a brand requires more than seven seconds of explanation then it is not a very good brand. I've reinvented yet again to Big Goals in Short Order. Now, the meeting planners who still have jobs get what I do and how I might help them. *Brand with a Unique Value Proposition (UVP)!*

- Fourth, when you jump into the marketplace deliver a Return on Investment (ROI). The days of speaking without accountability are all but gone. Answer this question for corporations, "How will you make me more money?" If your answer is not part of a UVP, then you are in the red ocean,* fighting and clawing for engagements. *Deliver ROI!*

> **WEBSITE REFERENCE TOOL**
>
> **www.speakerlauncher.com ➡**
> **Book Buyer LOGIN** *(red button)*
>
> **Recommended Reading:** W. Chan Kim's book, *Blue Ocean Strategy.*

Tips from the Masters: *VICTORIA LABALME*

MAKING YOUR SPEECH COME ALIVE:
Turning a Presentation into a Memorable Performance

- **Abandon All Ideas of What You Think a "Professional Speaker" Is or Should Be** — In addition to providing them with entertainment and a few innovative, practical ideas, there is nothing the audience wants more than the real, honest, authentic you. If your voice, demeanor, rhythm of speech, tonality or personality on the platform changes from who

---

* Red Ocean is a reference from *Blue Ocean Strategy* by W. Chan Kim and Renée Mauborgne (Harvard Business Review Press, 2005).

you are and sound like off the platform, you are in trouble. Audiences can smell phony speaker a convention room away.

- **Craft Your Presentation Keeping in Mind a "Dramatic Line"** — Design your keynote, speech or presentation based on the experience you want your audience to be having at any given moment. Consider not only your content, but the effect your delivery of that content will have on the audience. Think in terms of experience, effect and result, and position your speech/presentation segments in an order that will take the audience on a memorable journey. Break down your keynote into segments of the audience's experience, much like a movie.

Moment	Bit	Experience
#1	ABC	Engaged/Surprised/Entranced/Wowed/Entertained
#2	QRX	Drawn in
#3	XYZ	Challenged

You should be very aware of what experience your audience is having at any given moment.

- **Craft Potent Stories and Anecdotes** — People rarely come up to a speaker three years after a given presentation and say, "I've been thinking about your fourth point on leadership." However, what they do say is, "You know, I still think about that story you told about raking leaves with your son." Human beings remember stories. It's why every culture has them and its why they last. The Bible was written in parables, not points.

- **Take Advantage of Horizontal and Vertical Space** — Use the entire platform. Move to different areas for different stories. Most speakers do one of three things: stand in one spot, roam aimlessly, or pace along the edge of the platform like a caged animal. Consider all quadrants, especially those off to the side and far away in the corner ("upstage" left and right). If you are going to stand in one spot or walk in a line, make sure it's by design, not default.

- **Re-Live Your Stories** — Every time you tell a story, re-experience it. This is how Broadway actors can do eight shows a week and keep it fresh. Act from within. Relive the moments. If you make it real for you, it will be real for the audience.

- **Match Your Voice with the Experience** — Let your tone, pacing, rhythm and volume match your content. If you are telling the audience about being in the desert at night and you want to say "it was so quiet," make your voice almost a whisper on the word "quiet" and slow the pacing down, so you give the sense of the experience.

- **Act Out Your Characters** — Adjust both your voice and body for the personalities in your speech (receptionist, daughter, husband, mother, ticket agent, boss, etc). Many speakers will go far enough to make a slight adjustment to their voice, but few actually also change their physicality. When both are done together, a third synergistic element kicks in, and you will start to become a whole new character. Commit and go all the way. Take risks. Inhabit your characters. Audiences love this and appreciate a small performance. It's why they pay actors the big bucks.

- **Let Your Points Land** — And wait for the audience to "reply." Although you are the only one talking, your speech is not a monologue, but a dialogue. Your partner is the audience. They "speak" their part by absorbing, listening, laughing, applauding, processing. If you offer them an idea, make sure you give it time to "land." Avoid being a tennis ball machine, shooting out ideas non-stop. You are not an information dispenser. You are a caring human being who has something to share.

- **Pausing** — Speakers are often told to pause, but then they pause in ... the ... middle ... of ... a sentence ... and speed throughotherkeymoments. This makes no sense at all. The moment to pause is after a significant point, a complex idea, a passage of suspense or a change in topic. This gives the audience time to process what you have just said.

- **Craft Descriptions with Potent, Image-rich, Visual Words** — Use clever, insightful, creative words that make the images come alive. As Marceal Marceau once said, "The audience cannot see what you do not give them to see." The phrase "a shriveled, moth-like woman with dark glasses and fire-engine red lipstick" is considerably different from "an old woman." Use well placed metaphors and similes. All this said, avoid flowery language that makes you sound like you should be writing for Hallmark or your grandmother's embroidery pillow. Also, make sure each word adds a new dimension.

- **Typing and Talking** — Write your speech by typing it and by talking it. It's best to develop your material by doing both — live on your feet (even if that means in front of your living room wall) and also sitting at the computer. Speeches that are written entirely by pen or keyboard tend to sound stilted. The spoken and written word are two different art forms. If you've crafted a series of complex, verbose sentences with words and phrasing that are not organic to you, you're going to feel and sound awkward when you give your speech. Be sure that you are constantly moving between page and stage and that you are finding an organic, comfortable blend of the two.

- **Practice** — Practice, practice, practice. The rehearsal to performance ratio for dancers, actors, musicians, and athletes ranges anywhere from 10:1 to 500:1. For most speakers, it's 1:1. *There is absolutely no excuse for not rehearsing.* Rehearsing, however, does not mean memorizing your speech. In fact, memorizing (except for key elements in the opening and closing) is generally not a good idea, as you might begin to sound canned. Rehearsing means going over, out loud, any kind of difficult transition, story, point or moment. Practice also will decrease your nervousness as this is often a result of feeling out of control and unprepared. Practice in micro segments as opposed to large chunks. This makes rehearsing less intimidating, more manageable, and a lot more fun.

- **If You're Losing the Audience** — Don't rush! Most speakers make the mistake of thinking they ought to hurry through the rest of their material if the audience starts to get restless.

This will have an adverse effect: you'll lose them faster. The best thing to do is: 1) slow down to draw them in; 2) change the order of your final segments or insert a bit to make things more lively; 3) walk out into the audience — this always wakes people up; and 4) have them do something interactive or physical.

2.0 SPEECH TIPS (Victoria Labalme)

There's a lot of new technology out on the market and a lot of excitement around social media, but no matter how snazzy your technology, how swift your social media, or how high your production value, nothing can replace superb structure, content, and delivery and a truly well crafted message. Make sure your various forms of technology support your presentation rather than detract from it. Being too flashy on stage is a bit like a woman wearing a lot of vibrant clothing to attract attention. Natural beauty is timeless; and natural beauty in a presentation stems from what I call the Through Line™ — the driving force behind your work; your noble intent. Is your Through Line to show off or is it to connect with the audience? Make sure it's the latter and build your masterwork from there.

Master Victoria Labalme *is a performer and advanced performance coach who works with entrepreneurs, executives, authors and professional speakers, to strip away inorganic behavior and allow their true, authentic, voice to emerge.*

2.0 OTHER PEOPLE'S MATERIAL — OPM

It's easy when you get out there speaking to forget where you got some of your material. I did this and boy do I feel bad about it! In my talks to NSA and CAPS Chapters, I have been referencing the "through line" of the speech. Although I've used the term a bit differently, I totally forgot that I had first heard this term from Victoria. It wasn't until I was reworking this book that I realized I had been making a mistake. Victoria had been using the term Through Line™ as a core to her brand and a key concept in her material for years. My apologies to Victoria.

I believe this is a good teaching moment. Do you know where all of your ideas and material for your content have come from? Are you being careful to credit people who may have initiated an idea?

You know that quote from Marianne Williamson? "Our deepest fear is not that we are inadequate. Our deepest fear is that we are powerful beyond measure. It is our light, not our darkness that most frightens us. We ask ourselves, Who am I to be brilliant, gorgeous, talented, fabulous? Actually, who are you *not* to be?" Nelson Mandela used this is his inaugural speech and the quote started to become attributed to him. These things can happen so easily.

> *We all owe it to our profession to be more conscious of the origin of our materials.*

HOW IMPORTANT IS IT THAT THE SPEECH IS GOOD?

It's the only thing that matters. It's everything. No fancy six color brochure or flash website can overcome a mediocre speech.

"Be Good" Marketing

There are really two types of speaker marketing. One I like to call "be good" marketing and the other includes the traditional types of marketing such as websites, videos, print, social media, etc. We'll discuss traditional marketing when we take aim in Phase II.

> *No fancy six color brochure can overcome a mediocre speech.*

Amanda Gore moved to the U.S. from Australia many years ago with a handful of speeches on her calendar. She had been speaking in Australia for 16 years and was considered one of the best in her home country. Her speech was solid. High energy, funny, edgy — it had all the right components. Amanda spoke to just a few groups and took off like a rocket. Her marketing materials had little to do with her success. After every presentation several people would say, "I have a group that absolutely needs to hear your message" and it just kept happening over and over until Amanda's calendar was full. Amanda is the perfect example of "Be Good" marketing. She created a buzz in the industry that has continued and now, many years later, she is one of the busiest, highest paid female (or male) speakers in the U.S. She is definitely a Wealthy Speaker and you'll hear how she got her speech to be so great in her Flashpoint story later in this chapter.

Industry Green Monsters

Some time you might be sitting in an audience, seeing a speaker you've heard raves about, and think, "What's all the fuss about?" You think they are just okay.

Ask yourself this question, "Am I simply feeling jealous?" Believe me, it's common in this industry despite the fact that we are a group of highly evolved and well-adjusted individuals. People get jealous — no big deal. But rather than comparing your style to those doing well or allowing yourself to go to the Green Monster side, ask yourself some further questions.

- What can I learn from this speaker?
- What can I appreciate about their style? You don't have to change your style to be like them, but you do need to ask the question.
- What is it about their style that the audiences and meeting planners love?
- What is it that I would not do? What's just not me?
- Why do they keep booking them? What is special about their service beyond the speech?
- What do I need to do to create a buzz about my speech?
- Am I being honest about my level of talent?
- How can I take my speech to the next level while staying true to myself?
- What steps can I take to get to the Wealthy Speaker level?
- What steps can I take to reach my five or ten year goals?

COACH'S QUESTION: *Am I constantly comparing myself to other speakers? How is this serving me?*

So How Do I Know if I'm Really Good?

Many speakers use evaluations and they average five smiley faces out of six. Also people line up at the end of the program to say, "Thanks, that was awesome!"

A speaker friend of mine sat at the back of a meeting room waiting for his turn to speak. They were taking a short break and then the speaker before him would wrap up. He went into the washroom and heard two guys complaining that the material was fairly outdated and they weren't impressed. The meeting resumed and the speaker finished his talk. The two guys from the washroom were the first two in line to say to the speaker, "Hey, great job, thanks so much." So what does this tell us? Use evaluations and comments from the audience to build confidence, but do not take that to mean you are great and have no room for improvement. The number one way to know if you are really good is when people hand you their business card after the speech and say, "I've got a group that needs to hear that exact message."

> *The number one way to know if you are really good is when people hand you their business card after the speech and say, "I've got a group that needs to hear that exact message."*

If you are not getting an average of two or three spin-off gigs from each speaking engagement, then you need to go back to work on the speech. Find yourself a speech coach, books, CDs, training, whatever it takes. Continually hone your speech and it will pay off for you in the ultimate reward of more engagements.

2.0 IS THE SPEECH GOOD?

When people hand you their business card with spin-off ideas, the goal is that they are actually wanting to pay you! When people continually ask you to speak for free, this is telling you something — they are not valuing your work or you are getting in front of audiences that cannot take you anywhere.

⚡ FLASHPOINT: Amanda Gore, CSP, CPAE

I am not sure I have a specific flashpoint ... more a series of them really. The first came 20 years ago when my mentor said to me, "The most important thing is for you to have fun. When you have fun, your audience can have fun." That has held me in good stead ever since. He told me that very early on! Ron Tacchi, the same mentor, also told me to stop being a missionary! I was so passionate about people taking my messages on board because I knew that they would be healthier and happier if they did ... although I vehemently denied being a missionary. In retrospect, I was! And then I realized that my job was to bring the information, ideas, and skills to them in the best way I could. I had to allow them to choose what was best for them and what had an impact on them and let go of what I wanted them to do. That made a difference. An extension of that idea came when I started praying before I went on stage and imagined God's presence in the room ... and that I would be a vehicle for whatever was needed. I had no knowledge of what impact there might be and no attachment to it. My job was just to be the best I could be and to be of service to them in any way they needed. So I have always tried to have fun, be the best I can be, serve the audience as much as I can, and pray for them to be given what they need during the session.

2.0 AMANDA GORE

When I returned home to Australia after being gone for eight years, I had to create a new website. There were a lot of new hot speakers here, so I did what I did in the U.S. and worked very hard to be the best I could be. I'm happy to report that it worked and I'm blessed to be where I want to be. I am limiting myself to six presentations a month so I have a life! And two trips to the U.S. a year and I'm happy to report that the wonderful bureaus there still support me.

You'll hear a little more from Amanda in Chapter 7 in the section, Hiring Staff Who Are Winners.

GOOD SPEAKERS VERSUS GREAT SPEAKERS

Television shows like *American Idol* can teach us a lot. Once you've watched the show a few times, you start to see the difference between good singers and great singer/performers. With some exceptions, the singers who are booted off closest to the end are the ones that are truly great.

Figure G provides a big picture list of the traits of good speakers versus the traits of great speakers.

FIGURE G: **Good Versus Great Speakers**

GOOD	GREAT
Speak on many topics	Are known for one thing
Business is affected significantly by the economy	Business is steady growth consistently
Take most/all business that is offered	Accept only the business that is right for them — refer the rest to other experts
Compare themselves to others	Revel in their uniqueness and learn from people they admire
Get told they are great speakers but wish they had more business	Get two to three spin-off gigs from each engagement
Have testimonials saying they are great speakers	Have testimonials saying how the audience or the company changed as a result of their talk
Have style or substance	Have both style and substance (some exceptions apply)
Advertise in industry magazines	Are columnists in industry magazines
Buy a booth at trade shows	Are the headline keynote at trade shows
Get a standing ovation sometimes and revel in them	Don't put much stock in standing ovations whether they get them or not
Show up to give "their" speech	Make it about the audience, not themselves

GOOD	GREAT
May lack clarity on the value they bring	Know exactly who they are, the value they bring and walk the world with that confidence
Get asked to negotiate fees	Clients will pay what the expert charges
Business runs them	They run their business efficiently in a way that is perfect for them

These guidelines are loaded with some exceptions, but think of them as goals to aim toward. Alan Weiss is a great example of a speaker who moved to the *expert* side.

Peter Legge Works the Tradeshow

The second speaker I represented was Peter Legge, CSP, CPAE, out of Vancouver. He was a brilliant keynote speaker and got a lot of spin-off from each engagement. He was so easy to sell and he had a great demo video. One summer we went to a trade show in Seattle that was an industry event for meeting professionals. Peter spoke at the breakfast in the morning and did a fabulous job. The audience was told that he would be at our trade show booth in the afternoon and that there would be a surprise for them at the booth. We brought enough books to give one to every meeting planner and we asked them to fill out a quick form in order to collect their book. Peter was at the booth autographing and I was collecting the forms. We asked them three key questions:

1. How many events do you run each year where you use outside speakers?
2. What is your average speaker budget? We gave them four tiers to choose from: 0–$2,500; $2,500–$5,000; $5,000–$7,500; and $7,500 +.
3. When is your next event?

Everyone filled out the form and we attached their business card. We got everything we wanted for the cost of 100 books (hard cost of about $3.00 per book). I followed up diligently and that event turned into about 25 pieces of spin-off business over the next two years. It was so easy. Think about how you might take this idea and apply it to an event you are doing in the next 12 months. Meeting planners will often offer you trade-show booths and other great things — you just have to ask.

2.0 TRADESHOWS

Standing all day at a tradeshow booth puts you into the category of "sales person" rather than "expert." If you secure a booth as a part of your deal, do your best to use your booth wisely and to differentiate. Think outside of the booth. Most tradeshow booths are a giant waste of time because people don't know how to network properly and have people engage with them. Perhaps you meet people at your booth for an autograph session at a particular time after your keynote?

If you've secured a tradeshow booth as part of your gig, think outside the booth.

Fees — How Much Should I Charge?

When you are in the early stages of your career, this question can be very confusing. At the NSA meetings (in the U.S. only) we are not able to discuss fees — for legal reasons (I believe it's because they don't want to be accused of collusion).

A professional speaker is someone who makes a living at delivering presentations. And it's with that in mind that I say the following: If you aren't charging at least $1,500 per presentation, then in my mind you are not yet a professional speaker. I always emphasize value when talking about fees because knowledgeable meeting planners know what the market offers and whether or not you are in line.

Many people are out in the workforce gaining knowledge for ten or twenty years before they deliver one keynote. The client is paying for two things — your unique perspective on a topic and your delivery of that perspective. Consider also that clients are not just paying for

Consider that clients are not just paying for that one hour of your time, but the years of experience that go into your expertise.

that one hour of your time, but the years of experience that go into your expertise.

Your content and your delivery style will be what shoots your fee up the ladder quickly. I've seen speakers with very basic content go extremely far in this industry because of their style. One example is Keith Harrell's "Attitude is Everything." Speakers have been talking about attitude for years but Keith makes it fresh to his audiences. Keith's delivery astounds people. He is as motivational as they come and that's what clients pay for. The corporate world pays millions of dollars each year to keep their employees motivated — to change their attitudes. Keith Harrell has carved out a fabulous niche for himself with a fairly simple topic and even landed himself a full-page spread in the *Wall St. Journal* talking about the importance of attitude.

2.0 KEITH HARRELL UPDATE

I'm sad to say that we lost Keith Harrell to illness a few years ago. He was a force to be reckoned with in this industry and a huge loss. If you would have asked me 20 years ago "Can a speaker build a career on a topic like 'attitude,'" I would have said, "Hell no!" But Keith showed us that you could own a word like "attitude," which some might consider fluffy, and build a huge career on it.

TIPS ON SETTING AND RAISING FEES

Assigning a dollar value to yourself is not an easy task. Many factors come into play — some relevant and some not. Below are some pointers for setting fees and knowing when and how to raise them.

- Start somewhere. Do your homework, ask clients and other speakers and set a fee. It may be low to begin, but there's only one way to go — Up! You can raise it as you build your confidence and momentum.

- If you have any level of celebrity status — you write a column, do a national radio show, wrote a book that's gotten some attention, etc. — then you can start higher than average. If you've come out of a high-level corporate position, that may also put you at a higher starting position.

- Put your fees down on paper in the form of a fee schedule and post it on your bulletin board in your office. Don't pull a different number out of the air every time a client calls. If you do seminars as well as keynotes, have them all listed on the page. You may use this internally in the beginning, but eventually you'll want to make a fee schedule available for your clients upon request. Everything that the client will need to set a budget should go on this page — include such items as speaking fees, travel expenses, AV requirements, etc.

- Don't post your fee schedule on your website. You want to have an opportunity to establish value with your clients long before fee is discussed.

- Never charge more than your fee just because you think a client has more money. If you want to capture more of their budget, do it with additional value — programs or product — but keep your fee integrity.

- Travel expenses are typically separate. Some speakers offer a travel inclusive fee or a flat fee for travel. The benefit of a flat fee is that the client is never surprised. You don't want your last communication with your client to be negative due to an issue with travel expenses.

- A great way to gauge if you are ready to raise your fees is when these situations arise: your clients tell you that you are too inexpensive, your calendar is getting full, you just released a new book or product that gains attention, or you're sharing the stage with much higher priced speakers.

- Test your fee idea with the people who book you the most (i.e., bureaus, clients).

- Harry Beckwith in "Selling the Invisible" talks about meeting a little fee resistance. If you are not meeting any resistance at all, your fee may be too low.

- Make sure that you are always giving more value than your fee. Your client should feel more than satisfied.

- Know what's going on in the market. Don't be afraid to ask people what they charge. It might surprise you.

- Don't allow fear to dictate your decisions. When you raise your fee, be prepared to lose 25% of your business from the bottom end, but know that you should gain 25% better clients at the top. Make room for those better clients in your business.

FEES ARE A STATE OF MIND

Fees are a state of mind. When a client calls you, is your gremlin running the show or are you? Either you believe (inside and out) that you are worth your fee or you don't. Has this conversation ever taken place for you?

> **Client:** I'd like to book you.
>
> **You:** Great! (*inside voice: "I wonder if they can afford me?"*)
>
> **Client:** What do you charge?
>
> **You:** $5,000 (*inside voice: "Geez, they're never going to pay that much!"*)
>
> **Client:** Can we negotiate?
>
> **You:** Well, uh, maybe …

Of course they are going to negotiate. Your inside voice, the gremlin, is running the show! I'll say it again: Fees are a state of mind. When you first establish value and stand tall in your fees and state them with confidence, then people are less likely to try to negotiate. Now, there's the odd person that just has to ask for a deal, but for most, this is true. Here's how the conversation should go:

> **Client:** I'd like to book you, how much do you charge?
>
> **You:** Well, I'm not sure that I'm a fit for you. First, tell me a little about where you need help.
>
> **Client:** Our people are being asked to do more with less and they are starting to burn out.
>
> **You:** Great, I think I would be able to address that with my presentation called "XYZ." Some of the benefits of XYZ are that your people will … (*go on to describe the benefits and the return on investment*).

Client: That sounds like exactly what we need. What is your fee?

You: I charge $5,000 for a keynote and $6,500 if you add a breakout session the same day. (Now you shut up ... be quiet ... no if, ands, buts.)

Client: Great — I'll run that past Mr. Jones and get back to you.

You: In the meantime, let me send you an e-mail with my website information, so you can review it and forward it on to Mr. Jones too.

Did you see the difference? First we want to establish value, then we can talk fee. And most importantly, once you quote your fee, be quiet. If they come back to you with a counter-offer, then you would go to your list of reasons to negotiate your fee (see negotiating fees below) and see if they qualify. If they don't, then be willing to give up that piece of business. You'd be surprised how often people will say no and then come back to you later. They are somehow committed to you once they've made a choice and often find a way to make it work. You might offer to throw in some books to help close a deal. Sometimes, they just want to know that you will "play ball" with them.

Attracting Your Perfect Client

When I first got into the coaching field, I didn't know what to charge clients. I knew that my expertise was worth something, but I wasn't sure how much. I was trained at CTI (The Coaches Training Institute) and I heard a lot of fees mentioned — most of them I thought were extremely low. I asked the instructor what fees he was charging. He was at the top of the industry. That was the figure I was shooting for, but I set my fee below his. I had to start somewhere. I have since quadrupled that fee, blew past the instructor and it will continue to go up. Every time I raise my fees, I attract a more perfect group of clients. And after several years, only two people have ever asked to negotiate my fees. Why? Because my mind is not open to it. I don't make it an option. I'll talk more about attracting your perfect clients in Chapter 5, under The Attraction Method. Basically, I attract clients who can easily afford my coaching and you should be attracting clients who can easily afford your fee as well.

Side Note About Fees

Walking the halls of NSA conventions can yield interesting perspectives. You often overhear a speaker boasting how he did 150 gigs last year. What the listener rarely asks is "at what fee?"

Many speakers (not all) who are delivering more than 100 engagements per year are charging relatively low fees. Don't fall into the trap of speaking yourself to death just so that you can say a big number to your colleagues. Trust me when I say that 100 gigs per year is not a great number if you want to lead any sort of a life outside of your business, especially if you have children. Raise your fees and speak less. You'll lose 25% of your business at the bottom and gain a better 25% at the top. Speak less and lead a more balanced life. Don't let fear of raising your fee dictate the level of balance in your life. You do need to "make hay while the sun is shining," just make it at a higher profit! (See Cary Mullen's 2.0 update in Chapter 6 for more on lifestyle).

NEGOTIATING FEES

Write down specific reasons why you might negotiate your fee and tack them to your bulletin board. Then, stick with them. If a client does not meet your negotiation criteria, stick to your guns. Here are some possible reasons to negotiate your fee:

- multiple engagements;
- piggyback engagements — you are already in their city and can do more than one client in a period of time;
- they use you multiple times during their conference — many speakers offer a special price for a keynote plus a breakout in the same day — put that on your fee schedule to inspire clients to use you more;
- it's a charity that you want to support;
- there's a major opportunity for book sales; or
- it's a major meeting of your perfect target audience.

Every meeting planner will tell you that their engagement is great exposure. Don't take their word for it, do your homework on the group before you make the decision. Ask to talk to speakers whom they hired in years prior to see if the opportunity is as good as it sounds.

Avoid negotiating every time with speakers' bureaus. They are sales people. Therefore a part of their job is selling to the client and then selling you on the opportunity. Once you set the stage that you are open to negotiating on a regular basis — you are opening up a can of worms. Tell them your criteria and ask them to respect it.

Many meeting planners will work with more than one speakers' bureau to find the speaker they need for an event. This is another reason why you have to be very, very careful when negotiating fees with bureaus. Two bureaus could easily have submitted your name and if they are quoting two different fees then the situation could become sticky very quickly.

> *Bottom line about fees:* Make sure that you are always giving more value than your fee; don't be afraid to raise your fee (remember the 25% loss rule); and, most importantly, negotiation is a state of mind.

2.0 FEES

The recent economic shift has changed our industry. Things that used to occur in what we now refer to as "the good old days" may be gone forever. The days of the $10,000 speaker working 80 dates a year are not as common. Can it still be done? Sure, but perhaps not as frequently as before.

What's really changed and may never go back is the expectations of meeting planners and corporate executives. They used to have a healthy respect for speaker fees, whereas now they expect more value. So what do we do with this? Expect to be negotiated down and have a win-win card up your sleeve ready to play.

2.0 ORBITS OF THE SPEAKING WORLD

The graphic in Figure H will help you see how as a new speaker you might start out working and will graduate from orbit to orbit. Some may start right in the center, at the Rubber Chicken level, while others might launch straight into Making a Living. Everyone will move through the orbits differently. One of my clients started in his first year at Making a Living and has already hit the Sweet Spot within three years. Sweet! (See Flashpoint: Ryan Estis in Chapter 1 for his success!)

FIGURE H: **Orbits of the Speaking World**

RUBBER CHICKEN

The Rubber Chicken lunch or dinner circuit is where many speakers begin. These are the freebies that you give in order to get your momentum rolling. It's also a great opportunity to practice your speech. This might be your local associations, non-profits, and service clubs, like Rotary. Like I've said, some of you will never need to go this route. Just know it's an option.

SQUEAKING BY

A year or two into your business, you might be just barely cutting it, this is the Squeaking By phase. Your goal? To keep your momentum going and continue to raise your fees. You don't want to sit here too long. Be conscious about whether or not you are getting paid what you are worth. Some speakers spend years in this phase and then often give up. Either get really good and ask for what you are worth, or reconsider this industry.

MAKING A LIVING

The Making a Living phase is a nicer phase to be in. I realized that I've hovered there for a few years myself. The catalyst that got me moving again was realizing I wasn't living up to my potential. I believe I have the potential for greatness on all fronts — and I hope that you share this with me. Do you? That said, Making a Living might be exactly where you want to be. If you are balancing a family or taking care of elderly parents, this might be a perfect spot. However, if you feel that you are under-utilizing your potential, go for The Sweet Spot!

THE SWEET SPOT

Ahhhh, The Sweet Spot! It evens sounds great, doesn't it? This, I believe, is the ultimate for most speakers. You're earning a way-above-average living; you're living the lifestyle of your dreams; and you've got money for a rainy day. The Sweet Spot allows you to retire in extreme comfort.

THE SPEAKING CELEB

When you stop to think about it, we actually have quite a few people in our industry who would be considered celebrities. That doesn't mean they are household celebs like George Clooney or Condaleeza Rice, but they have name recognition within the corporate and association worlds. Some examples might be Harvey McKay, Brian Tracy, Les Brown, Jack Canfield, Larry Winget, Marcus Buckingham, Dan Pink, Seth Godin, Malcolm Gladwell, or Dan Heath. And I'd add people like Joe Calloway, Tim Sanders, and Mark Sanborn to that list. Notice the majority of these are authors whose books have done well.

What I think would surprise you is that these people put their pants on one leg at a time, just like you do. They, like you, have business issues to contend with and, no doubt, are constantly thinking about how they will remain relevant.

Stand tall in your confidence, stand tall in your expertise, stand tall in your fees!

BOTTOM LINE

With the constant challenges of our economy, we need to be prepared to add more value without diminishing our worth. Clients will appreciate someone who stands tall in their fees. And when we set out to attract clients who are perfect for us, they'll see our value and be willing to pay. Stand tall in your confidence, stand tall in your expertise, stand tall in your fees!

FLASHPOINT: Mark Sanborn, CSP, CPAE

Many sparks combined to ignite whatever success I enjoy today as a professional speaker and author. Here are three.

The first spark was the realization that a story is the most powerful communication tool in a communicator's repertoire. As a high school student I read Norman Vincent Peale and wondered why he told so many stories in his books. I just wanted the "meat and potatoes" — the how-tos. Over time I realized that stories are the mental coat pegs upon which listeners and readers hang ideas. Without a good story, a listener would not be emotionally impacted by the message or able to remember it easily.

Because of that, I focus heavily on looking for and developing unique stories with strong lessons. Telling the stories of others is far less effective than telling your own.

Another spark came out of my own interests and likes. While my background is in sales and marketing, that isn't where my passion lies. I know — and have always known — how to market and sell, but I would much rather develop material and speak. I discovered early that the better I was in front of an audience, the less I would have to beat the bushes for new clients. It is dramatically easier to sell a great speech than a mediocre one. I've always spent more time on developing my presentation and speaking skills than on clever ways to market and sell. (I do recognize that the only thing more powerful than being a great speaker is being a great speaker and a great marketer.)

The third spark is remembering that audiences love it when you understand them well enough to help them apply your ideas to their lives.

I started speaking full-time at the age of 27. Much of what compelled me to thoroughly research my audience and tailor my material was raw fear that I'd be thought an imposter. So I did my homework better than many of my competitors. As time went on, clients kept telling me how happy they were with my customization. "You sounded like you worked here" was high praise indeed.

Eventually I developed a system of consistently getting the information I needed to make my ideas and techniques specific to the day-to-day challenges of a particular audience. It isn't hard to learn enough about an audience to be well-informed. I may not understand the nuances of office politics, technological challenges, or vendor issues, but I can quickly know much about marketplace challenges, primary competitors, strategic practices, and the overall financial situation. The use of a well designed pre-program questionnaire, conversations with key decision makers and some Internet research allow me to effectively tailor and increase my relevancy to an organization.

All three of those sparks can help ignite your efforts if you use the ideas. The important point isn't what I've done or learned, but what you can learn and apply from my experience.

Those sparks — focusing on developing and using your own stories, being great on the platform, and understanding your audience and tailoring your material — are enough to ignite a rewarding and profitable career in professional speaking.

2.0 MARK SANBORN

I've been in this business of speaking full time for 25 years. What has changed?

The good news is that the Internet has given everyone a voice.

The bad news is that since the Internet has given everyone a voice, it is harder than ever to be heard.

In this competitive and over-crowded market space, it is not enough to be a great speaker. You need to be a great marketer, too. The combination of those two things — great marketing and a great performance — is what enables you to get heard. That means utilizing all the best tools for getting the attention of clients and getting them to choose you to speak.

And when you speak, you must deliver.

Great communicators don't just tell, they sell. They use the skill of writing catchy and compelling copy, not just for their presentations but for their sales and marketing efforts as well.

And what hasn't changed?

Despite all the exciting technologies and the opportunities they create, there is still no "magic bullet." You have to take responsibility for your own success and do the work. There are many other people and resources that can help and assist you, but they can't do it for you. That's your job. So roll up your sleeves and work harder and smarter than you've ever worked before. The payoffs will be gratifying.

If you think you're *ready*, if you have focused on your expertise, developed a great speech, and positioned yourself in the marketplace, you can move on to the next phase and take *aim*.

4

Phase II

AIM

Marketing to Reflect Positioning and Benefits

· ·

Taking the time in Phase I to focus on your speech and your positioning gets you *ready* to take *aim* at your marketing. Your marketing materials need to reflect the benefits of your presentation and your brand. I mentioned Amanda Gore's experience with "Be Good" marketing in the previous chapter, but here I'll show you the traditional marketing components you'll need to use to promote yourself — to get your name out there. Just because these are the traditional components doesn't mean you stop being creative and inventive.

> *No amount of marketing dollars can overcome a mediocre presentation.*

There is no better marketing than a great speech. Have I said that already? Hopefully I've said it several times because I want you to really take it to heart. No amount of marketing dollars, no fancy Facebook page, no ultra cool website can overcome a mediocre presentation. So if you don't think your speech is great, you need to go back and get *ready* before taking *aim*.

2.0 MARKETING MATERIALS

Everything about marketing has changed. Yester-year we used to use packets and one sheets, now we use websites as our primary marketing tool. Whereas before our "speaker" positioning was front and center, now we want to position as an expert who happens to speak.

What does that mean? If I go to your website and it says, "Hire me, I'm a speaker," I will be clicking away within seconds. If I go to your website and it says "These are the benefits and outcomes of our work and one of the ways that we deliver on those outcomes is speaking," now I'm listening. Whereas before you and your credibility were first, I believe the needs and the outcome for the client should be front and center now.

Today, the keys that should be universally apparent (that is, on every page) on your website are your name, your brand, and your promise.

2.0 COMPONENTS OF A GREAT MARKETING PIECE (WEBSITE)

There is an easy checklist that you can use to ensure that your marketing materials have all the right components. The formula makes it much easier to develop marketing materials that actually work — that is, result in bookings. I'll get into specific marketing pieces later in this chapter, but as an overview, here are the perfect dozen pieces.

1. Your Name
2. Brand
3. Promise Statement
4. Photos
5. Short Bio/Credibility
6. Return On Investment (ROI) Bullets
7. Powerful Questions
8. Testimonials
9. Client Lists
10. Reflect Your Essence
11. Uniqueness
12. Call to Action

YOUR NAME

Some of you may be aiming towards having a company that is bigger than you, something that you could sell to someone else. If that's the case, then you may not put your name right in the banner. But if you are the brand, and in some cases that may be the case, then don't forget to add it right from the start.

Always keep in mind that someone might search the Internet and come into your site on the "Contact Us" page. If that was the case, would they know within 15 seconds who you are and how you might help them? Many people overlook this and that's why having those three pieces (name, brand and promise) in the top banner or navigation area can be helpful.

The keys that should be universally apparent (that is, on every page) on your website are your name, your brand, and your promise.

YOUR BRAND

Some people may brand themselves (i.e., Dr. Phil) and some people may brand their work "Working in the Positive Zone with Susan Miller." Having an interesting brand can become a hook, "Hey, I wonder what working in the positive zone means?" Then, when paired with a solid promise like Susan Miller's "Creating a High Energy, Low Stress Workplace," you get it. A brand may not necessarily stand alone, but when combined with a solid promise, it should make perfect sense.

There are some terrific brands in our industry. Mark Bowden's "TruthPlane" for instance. You might not know what that means until you see his promise to "Connect with Your Audience, Command Attention and Convey the Right Message" and when you read further that it's about communication and presentation skills, it all becomes crystal clear.

YOUR PROMISE STATEMENT

This is your big picture — one line — that shows the meeting planner the results of your expertise. Examples might be: "Turning Managers into Leaders," "Leading Teams Through Change," "Boosting Small Business Growth," etc. My promise for my coaching company is "Catapulting Your Speaking Business." This is probably the hardest thing you will have to define. To get to this one sentence, turn to Coaching Exercise 8.

PHOTOS THAT REFLECT YOU

How many times have you looked at a website to see either no photo at all or a photo that does not reflect the personality of that speaker? Who you are is such an important piece of the buying puzzle. The meeting planner wants to know who you are and the minute they go onto your website, they should be able to get a sense of you. We've heard it said that photos are the windows to our souls and, before a buyer spends thousands of dollars, they want to see what you are all about. They are either looking for reasons to qualify you and take you to the next step or disqualify you and put you in the no-go pile.

Your photo answers some important questions:

- Are you fun?
- Are you confident?
- Are you a good person?
- Do you have integrity?
- Do you have great energy?

At least a portion of all buying decisions are made based on gut feeling. Whether a planner knows it or not, they trust their instincts a great deal and your photo is the first checkpoint that will either take you to the next phase or not.

Some of the No-Nos

Don't use staged (in studio) photos of yourself with a microphone, pointing a finger, in the superman pose, old hair styles or glasses, anything that could be deemed cheesy. What worked ten years ago, does not work today — especially in photography.

Women and men who change their hairstyles often have to ensure that their photo reflects who they are today. If you are worried about looking old it may be because you are old looking. Update your look if needed, but don't try to hide the person you are today.

SHORT BIO/CREDIBILITY

A full-blown bio can go onto your website on the About You page, but on the home page of your website you are going to need to draw out the highlights of your credibility. Remember — expert first, speaker second.

This section should answer the question, "Why is this person credible to deliver this message?" Unless you are speaking on family values, your short bio is not the place for information like where you live with your family and your hobbies. Save that for the long version.

Be as specific as possible to show the reader how your background prepared you to speak on this topic.

RETURN ON INVESTMENT (ROI) BULLETS

In the example in Coaching Exercise 8, we've already drawn out what some ROI bullets might look like. ROI bullets answer the question, "What will change as a result of your work?" They need to be meaty, specific, and concrete.

Consider a good bullet to be something like: "Your team will learn how to quickly diffuse conflict and difficult situations" as opposed to "Your team will work better together." Really go into the nuts and bolts of what you are teaching in order to build your ROI bullets.

POWERFUL QUESTIONS

They teach us in coaching school that our best weapon is a powerful question. Providing a list of questions, a quiz, or an audit for your clients will help them discover how much they need you. A quiz (say, ten questions) might be best placed on your website; whereas, on your one sheet, you might only ask two or three of the most powerful questions.

The phrase, "How would your company be different if ..." followed by a list of things that you list as ROI could and should peak the interest of the meeting planner, especially if you are hitting a hot-button need for them. A hot-button need is something that they are struggling with right now. Ideally, the market should be full of people who have the need that you are offering to fill.

Let's use Barbara, from Coaching Exercise 8, as an example — she's turning managers into leaders.

Would your company be run more effectively if:

1. Your managers were strong communicators;

2. Your managers made better decisions;

3. Your managers hired winners who performed at high levels;

4. Your managers were consistently taking on more responsibility and operating at higher levels of efficiency; and

5. Your managers were strong, confident leaders.

The goal is for anyone who takes the quiz to immediately think, "Yes, we need this!"

TESTIMONIALS

Please excuse me if I slip into rant mode here for a minute.

Testimonials are one of the marketing tools that speakers rarely use effectively. Do I mean that speakers don't supply their clients with enough testimonials — No! I mean that every speaker is using the same testimonial letter as every other speaker. Let me give you an example of a lousy testimonial.

Testimonials are one of the marketing tools that speakers rarely use effectively.

Dear John Smith,

Thank you for participating in our 4th Annual Sales Awards Banquet. Our meeting was a huge success largely due to you.

Our audience loved your presentation and the comments are still rolling in. You are truly a great speaker, John.

Thanks again,
Joanne Nugent
Sales Manager

This is a lovely vanilla flavored letter, but it's not telling the prospective client anything that he or she hasn't heard a zillion times before. You are a good speaker — so what! So is everyone else.

What you want for testimonials is for them to answer the question: "What changed as a result of John Smith's presentation?" That's what you need to ask your client to write about. *You are a good* Some speakers design the letter for the client; *speaker — so what!* some ask for a two-line testimonial over e-mail. *So is everyone else.* I think if you can get it on letterhead, it would be helpful. It's nice to scan the logo of the company along with the two lines and use it all on your website (provided you obtain their permission). So here's what you do want:

> Dear John Smith,
>
> Oh my goodness, people are still buzzing about your presentation during sales meetings, at the water cooler, even in the employee washrooms! The phrase "Close it with love" has been posted on bulletin boards and walls all over our building and in our other three offices as well. Every week, we start our sales meetings with the alignment technique that you shared with us and after only 30 days, we have seen a 15% rise in sales.
>
> You are unbelievable, John. Thank you so much for making our company a better place to work and, more importantly, a more desirable company to do business with!
>
> We'll see you in April for that follow up program we discussed.
>
> > Thanks again,
> > Joanne Nugent
> > Sales Manager

Do you see the difference between Example 1 and Example 2? Night and day. Every speaker has a drawer full of Example 1, so by getting some more potent testimonials, you will have yet another way to differentiate yourself.

Strategically Place Your Testimonials

Whether it be in your print materials or on your website, try to place your testimonials immediately following a statement that you have made. You might put a testimonial that backs up your promise statement within close proximity. Every time you make a claim, have a testimonial from someone else to back it up. Every speaker might say that they are high energy and humorous, so have a testimonial that helps go that one step further and says why the energy and humor was effective with that group.

Testimonials don't have to be three paragraphs long, one to two lines can be super effective.

CLIENT LIST

Consider the types of engagements that you are trying to book and have your client list reflect that plan. For instance if you are trying to book international conferences of associations, then you don't want a list that has a lot of local corporate work. Many speakers look too small or too local in their client list. If you do the National Association of Financial Analysts, Madawaska Chapter — just list it as National Association of Financial Analysts. Now, don't get me wrong, I'm not asking you to lie. Lying will almost always come back on you, but, I don't believe that you need to describe the circumstances of each and every event — the client name is sufficient.

In terms of a one sheet,* you'll need just a partial client list — no more than 20 names. On your website, however, you can list all of your clients. You may even organize them into industry categories.

An example of a good client list, one that shows a good variety of national and international organizations, may look like the one below.

> Bank One
>
> International Association of Technology Engineers
>
> Merrill Lynch
>
> National Association of Women Business Owners
>
> Boston University

A less effective client list, one that shows only local organizations, might look like the one below.

> Ann Arbor Realtors Association
>
> Ann Arbor High School

---

* See later in this chapter for an update on the use of one sheets.

Ann Arbor Junior Chamber of Commerce

Rotary Club of Ann Arbor

When you are first starting out, you'll need to go with what you have, but be sure that you can update your materials as your client list grows. A meeting planner who looks at hundreds of speakers each year knows what to look for on the client list, so make sure your list is actually adding to your credibility rather than taking away from it.

REFLECT YOUR ESSENCE

All of your marketing materials need to show and tell the reader who you are. Think of a number of terms that describe you and make a list for the people who are going to help you design your marketing materials. You might use words like: confident, professional, value oriented, honest, warm, etc.

So what are you all about? What's important to you? What colors resonate with you? Show your suppliers exactly who you are, so that they can reflect that in your marketing materials.

One exception to this might be if you plan to sell the company. You may not want your presence to be so front and center on your marketing materials. It will be more about the value that you offer.

DELIVERY STYLE/UNIQUENESS

It's not unusual to see several speakers' websites touting all of the same phrases: high energy, humorous, thought-provoking, etc. Try to delve further into your talent to come up with words that will differentiate your style. Really listen to what your audiences say to you after your presentations. They will often provide words that can be used in your marketing.

When using language that describes your presentation, try to use terms that can be associated directly back to you. For example, Jamie Renfrew's "Meet Me Halfway"™ technique is designed to bridge divides in your team and rebuild unity.

CALL TO ACTION

Every marketing piece you develop should explain to the reader what action you want them to take. Whether it be your website, print materials or video, they should all finish with a call to action. "Call today to find out how to Turn Your Managers Into Leaders" or "Contact us now to schedule your time with Sara Jones." It's not that the client can't figure it out, but we want to guide the process as much as possible. For instance the next step in your process might be a 15-minute conference call to determine if you are the right fit for the job. If so, then that's what you want them to do and all calls to action should state such.

Coaching Exercise 8: **GETTING TO YOUR PROMISE STATEMENT**

This line explains the big picture of your bottom line results. It shows the prospect the results of your expertise. Examples might be: "Turning Managers into Leaders", "Leading Teams Through Change," "Boosting Small Business Growth," etc.

The steps and the sample below give you an idea of the process. In the end you should have a short, powerful phrase that sums up what you do and who you do it for. Turn to the next page and create your own promise statement.

1. List all of the outcomes that take place as a result of your presentations.

2. Now that you have your list, ask the question, "If people do all of these things, what will they get?" Continue to ask until you have another list.

3. Take a look at the entire list, circle the best and most unique words, and try to sum it up in one sentence.

Your Promise Statement: Sample _____

Barbara speaks to managers about building their teams. So she lists all of the outcomes (ROI) that will result because of her presentation:

1. Managers communicate more clearly and purposefully with their teams.

2. Managers will hire, develop and retain high performers.

3. Managers will make better decisions more quickly.

4. Managers will take on higher levels of responsibility in the company.

Now she looks at this list. If managers do all of the above, what will that give them? She could bat this around for awhile, but one idea would be that managers lead better. Therefore the phrase might be "Moving from Manager to Leader."

Then she needs to check in with the market place. She needs to ask clients (preferably C-Suite executives), "How would your company be different if all managers were better leaders?" If they respond, "That would be fantastic," then she knows she is onto something.

Your Promise Statement _____

1. List all of the outcomes that take place as a result of your pre-
    sentations. What will change in the organization or individual
    as a result of being in your session?

    _____

    _____

    _____

    _____

    _____

2. Now that you have your list, ask the question, "If people do all
    of these things, what will they get?" Continue to ask until you
    have another list.

    _____

    _____

    _____

    _____

    _____

3. Take a look at the entire list, circle the best words, and try to
    sum it up in one sentence. Make sure that your promise state-
    ment is one that will appeal to meeting planners — something
    that makes them say, "Yes, we need that!"

    _____

    _____

    _____

    _____

    _____

You can also find all of these exercises in a separate and conveniently bound
workbook: *Wealthy Speaker Workbook and Planning Guide.*

Marketing Materials — What Do I Need Exactly?

The manner in which clients buy has changed over the years and will continue to change along with technology. The old method of marketing was called "call-send-call." You would call someone on the phone to see if they had a need. If they did, you would send them your marketing package which included a folder of print materials and a demo video. After a week or two, you would call back to follow up.

But now with technology in place, you might not even start out the same way. You might send someone an e-mail query (see Chapter 5 for a discussion of Cold Calls Versus E-mail Query) to establish whether or not there is a need. If you do call them, you might have them go to your website while on the phone, or you might send them an e-mail proposal once the phone call is complete. Ideally, of course, you want them to be calling because you've established yourself as an expert or because they were referred to you by a colleague. With this said, you need to prepare for all occasions and give them sufficient tools to book you.

To market effectively, you want to aim at three components.

- Website
- Video Samples
- Social Media

Your Website

There are three main areas to consider when building or updating a website:

1. **Image/Marketing** — Make sure your website produces the desired image and establishes you as an expert in your field.

2. **Traffic** — This includes not just getting people there, but making them a part of your community or orbit once they arrive. "Orbit" is a word that Bob Scheinfeld uses to talk about people who are on his e-mail list. Bob is a master at Internet marketing.

3. **Conversion** — Get them to buy a product or a service once they have visited.

WEBSITE GOALS

Your first step is to really get clear on the goals for your website. What is the big picture? What do you want to happen once people arrive? Many speakers use their website as an image tool only — probably not on purpose, but simply because they haven't taken the steps to build traffic or convert it. If your main purpose is to allow people to get a feel for you and your work, then this is fine, *but*, you could be missing out on some major income-generating opportunities.

Your website is your first line of offence when it comes to marketing. It's your image, it's your giant calling card, it's a chance to really Wow! the client. A large percentage of speakers' websites I've seen would not impress seasoned meeting planners, so I'm happy when I see people doing web overhauls and updates.

> **WEBSITE REFERENCE TOOL**
>
> **www.speakerlauncher.com** ➡
> **Book Buyer LOGIN** *(red button)*
>
> Check out some of the technology masters like Bob Scheinfeld, Randy Gage, or Tom Antion.

 ## WRITING CONTENT FOR YOUR WEBSITE

One of the most difficult tasks for a business owner is writing the copy on their website. The #1 reason for this? They have no focus. Typically you are thinking about serving three or four different markets when writing the site. Choosing one target market makes this process so much easier. You can serve your other markets by offering program titles that are more specific, but it's very helpful to write only for your primary target market.

It's very helpful to write only for your primary target market.

TECHNOLOGY IN PHASES

Getting educated on how traffic comes to your site and how to convert them into buyers is a heady and time-consuming process. Consider working on your website in phases. Many Internet marketing gurus will tell you that your web designer (the creative one) probably does not know very much about how search engines find your site. Hopefully you can find a designer that does know the scoop, but it's safe to say that you should educate yourself regardless. The process might look something like this:

- Phase I — Get a website education. Learn about traffic, search engines, key words, meta tags, etc.
- Phase II — Draft the content for your website and choose a web designer.
- Phase III — Get the website built. Stick with the basic components, and a name capture element (a way to gather names and e-mail addresses) and leave the bells and whistles for another phase.
- Phase IV — Test your site. Get feedback and make changes.
- Phase V — Make changes and add bells and whistles, such as quizzes, product pages, etc.
- Phase VI — Full blown launch to clients, search engines, etc.

One of the *main* reasons to have a website is to capture names and e-mail addresses. How well is your site doing this?

2.0 NAME SQUEEZE, DANGLING A STRONG CARROT

It's true. Without a name capturing mechanism, your website may be missing an important marketing tool. When you gather up names and e-mail addresses, you now have permission to market to these people using your auto-responder system.

The Carrot? Dangling a strong carrot means offering something of value — so much value that people will give up their most prized possession, their e-mail address. By saying "sign up for my newsletter" you aren't giving them any reason to sign up. Who wants yet another newsletter in their in-box? I bet I get ten newsletters a day — all unsolicited. By the way, if you aren't set up with a proper "unsubscribe" option, you are spamming. Don't to it. Get the tools in place to do this properly.

So what's a good carrot? It depends on your audience. If I was a leader looking for communication solutions, maybe a special report on "communication mistakes leaders make" might capture my attention. Or a video. Or a three-week course. You'll need to test your carrot and see if it works to get people to sign up.

Dangling a strong carrot means offering something of so much value that people will give up their most prized possession — their e-mail address.

WHAT TO INCLUDE ON YOUR SITE

Universal elements on your website, as I've mentioned before, should include your name, brand, and promise.

The most common tabs or pages on a speaker's website are outlined below. As always, I encourage you to be unique. This is simply a guide so that you know where to begin.

1. **Home Page.** This page should include the following:

   - Your name, unless you are planning to sell this company later. You are the figurehead and should be front and center;
   - Photo of you (potentially built into the banner);
   - Video of you speaking (see later in this chapter for more on this);
   - Photo of your book;
   - Brief paragraph that describes the problem (i.e., leaders don't communicate well and these are the results);
   - Paragraph that describes the solution (i.e., your formula for successful leadership communication);
   - ROI bullets;
   - Brief paragraph that describes your credibility (mini-bio);
   - Testimonial;
   - Quotes from you that establish you as the expert rather than quotes from Mother Theresa or Tom Peters; and

- Some thought-provoking questions for the reader. This might come in the form of a short quiz or audit and should lead the reader to understand why they need you.

The home page should really capture your essence and allow people to see who you are and how you are unique. Sometimes less in more on a home page, so you may not use all of these pieces on this page. Instead, you might scatter them throughout the website.

2. **Keynotes and Workshop Page.** This page lists your offerings and should be one of the first tabs on your list of options if your goal is to sell keynotes and workshops. If consulting or something else is your primary goal, then that should be your first tab or link.

The format for the program outlines page could be as follows:

- Title,
- Subtitle,
- One paragraph that describes the program,
- Bullet points describing the benefits of that program (ROI),
- One short paragraph that describes your style in presenting the program, and
- A testimonial that backs up your style.

To differentiate your programs, you might add a little piece that describes the "Best Audience" and "Program Formats."

Example: Leadership Communication: It's Not What You Say, It's How You Say It
45-90 minute keynote — Best Audience: Leaders and Managers (also available as a breakout session — up to 1 day)

3. **About You Page**. This is your bio page and can cover all of your credentials as well as some personal, fun stuff. Note, to

make this site about them first and you second, your About
You link should be *after* your offerings links (keynotes,
consulting, etc.) on your menu of options.

4. **Clients Page.** This page provides a client list and testimonials.
   I also encourage you to have testimonials on every page to
   back up your claims, as noted above on the programs page.

5. **Products Page/Store.** This is where you sell your books,
   etc. You should have a shopping cart on your website when
   you have two or more products to sell, but that is an entire
   beast onto itself. You might want to take it in stages.

6. **Free Stuff Page/Resource.** Your audiences can go to this
   page to get more information about your expertise, articles,
   etc. During your presentations you should be offering items
   that will lead the audience to your website, especially if you
   sell products online and not back of room.

   If you find you're getting too many navigation options,
   you might want to bury this within another area. Your main
   navigation buttons should be used for the most important
   pieces.

7. **Meeting Planners and/or Speakers' Bureau Page.** People
   go to this page to find out what they need before they book
   you (in the pre-engagement section) and where they can
   get what they need once they have already booked you. The
   pre-engagement section should provide links to download
   video, one sheet, programs, bio, etc. The "once they have
   booked you" section might include your pre-program questionnaire, downloadable photos, bio (for publication), AV
   requirements, list of product and quantity pricing, articles
   that they can use before and after your presentation and
   hand-out originals. Anything that a client might ask you for
   once a booking has been made.

8. **Contact Page.** This should typically be the last option on
   your menu or navigation bar. My advice is to make it as
   easy and painless as possible for a client to get in contact
   with you. Have your 1-800-number and e-mail on every

page if possible, but please don't ask the client to answer 25 questions in order to make contact with you. If you do want a form, ask for three things: name, e-mail, date of next meeting or reason for inquiry. And have your phone number and e-mail above that form so they have the option to circumvent the form. My pet peeve is not being able to find someone's email and phone number on their site.

9. **Instant Chat Option.** I've debated having this option available on my site and may still go ahead with it. Imagine your prospect being able to talk to someone live on their first contact with you. They might want to check a date or ask a question about fees. I would always try to tee up a phone call to discuss their needs first, but I think Live Chat via instant messaging (IM) might set you up as being unusual and different. Many of us might have our virtual assistant or staff person field the calls, which would leave us free for other things, but imagine how surprised a client might be to get you personally.

 COACH'S QUESTION: *How is my website unique? What can I do to separate myself from the pack?*

WHAT DOES NOT BELONG ON YOUR SITE

What should not appear on your site can be as important as what should appear. I have just one item that must be avoided — Fees. You want to talk to a client or prospect in person to get them excited about the idea of working with you. Never rely solely on technology to sell you. You want the opportunity to start to build a personal relationship. So always have fee conversations after you have established value and in person, rather than over e-mail.

RATE YOUR WEBSITE

Once you've defined your website goals, phased in the technology, and built the appropriate pages, you need to step back and rate your site. Try to put yourself in your client's position and look at things objectively. You may want to run a beta test and get some input from people you trust. Remember one of the main reasons to have a website is to capture names and e-mail addresses. How well is your site doing this? Use the rating form in Coaching Exercise 9 to set goals and make your changes in stages, if needed.

 ## WEBSITES

Websites have gotten a little out of hand when it comes to providing options for the visitor. For instance, many websites use drop-down lists off of their main tabs. And when you add it all up, the visitor has to decide from 35 options where to click first. It's too confusing! And remember that old saying, I think I heard it first from Bob Bly, "A confused buyer never buys." On top of that many people offer all of the social media tabs on their home page as well, which means even more options. And believe me, if I head off to Facebook or Twitter, you've lost me, so really think about where these might best fit on your site.

If the visitor has to decide from 35 options where to click first, it's too confusing. Remember: A confused buyer never buys.

Bottom line: Your website needs to show me within 15 seconds what you do and how you do it. So if I see your name, your brand and promise in the top banner, then I see keynotes and workshops, consulting, coaching, bookstore, etc., in the navigation options, then I know what you do and how you deliver it. Make sense?

Coaching Exercise 9: WEBSITE RATING FORM

Now that your site is built, step back and evaluate it. Try to put yourself in your client's position and look at things objectively. You may want to run a beta test and get some input from people you trust.

Rate yourself on a scale of 1 to 10 — 10 being perfect.

Many of these items will be found on your home page, but this references your entire website.

_____ First Impression — does my website look professional?

_____ Can the client easily determine what it is I do? Or do they have to dig?

_____ Are the benefits listed?

_____ Is my promise statement front and center?

_____ Is my photography reflective of who I am? Is it creative or the same as every other speakers'?

_____ Do I have a video with some strong speaking footage?

_____ Does my mini-bio make it clear why I am the expert to speak on this topic?

_____ Do I ask a powerful question or offer a quiz that helps people see why they might need my services?

_____ Are my testimonials strong enough? Do they answer the question: "What changed as a result of my services?"

_____ Is my client list impressive?

_____ Do I describe my uniqueness?

_____ Does the site reflect my personality, my values and my essence?

_____ Do I capture names and e-mail addresses effectively?

_____ Am I offering just a few places to click from my home page?

_____ Are my tab names clear so that people know what I offer?

_____ Do I have a strong call to action?

_____ Is it simple for clients to get in touch with me?

Anything you rated six or less will need work in the future. Plan ahead and make the changes in stages if you feel overwhelmed. Go back and review the website section again if you need more direction on any of these items.

You can also find all of these exercises in a separate and conveniently bound workbook: *Wealthy Speaker Workbook and Planning Guide.*

MANAGING YOUR WEBSITE

If you are at all tech savvy, then you may choose to manage the content on your website yourself. However, this isn't for everyone and many designers will tell you it's a bad idea because they don't want you messing with their HTML. You can manage your site without knowing much HTML. You'll save $25 to $150/hour *and* you'll have the freedom to be more creative. If your website content is more than 18 months old, it's most likely stale. Update, update, update.

Creativity is really the big one for me. When you get an idea in the middle of the night for a new initiative, you simply fire up your program (like Dreamweaver or Adobe Contribute) and within minutes your idea comes to life on the screen and is live for the world to see. I've done it both ways and I felt ten times more in control of my business once I took over my website. I was writing all the time, which meant I was more plugged in. I had my designer set up the process so that I could update the copy content. Any changes to the graphics, my designer did for me.

If your website content is more than 18 months old, it's most likely stale. Update, update, update.

2.0 MANAGING YOUR WEBSITE

Great news on this front. Most websites are being based in Wordpress platforms now, which means that we can easily go in and change up our content without enlisting a web designer. Learning Wordpress is pretty easy and you may still want to have someone in charge of the site, handling your graphics portions for you.

Homemade materials look homemade.

I have a Wordpress person on my team and most of my sites have now been converted to Wordpress. I'll have a professional design the banner and the templates and then I'll go in and lay down all of the content.

Print Materials

• •

Unless you are a graphic designer by trade, you will want to hire an expert when it comes to establishing the look of your print materials. Homemade materials look homemade.

WHAT BASIC PIECES DO I NEED?

If you are marketing directly to meeting planners only, and not to speakers' bureaus (see Chapter 6 for Speakers' Bureaus), then it is debatable whether you need print materials at all. And even now, Speakers' Bureaus mostly use websites and/or electronic materials. You might consider making the pages listed below on your website "printer friendly," so that when meeting planners in a committee are considering you, they can pass around the pages within the group.

• Bio page
• Keynotes and Workshops page
• Home page

2.0 ONE SHEETS

I am against developing print materials unless you have a specific use for them, such as a direct mail program. I love the idea of a post-card, for example. You must know your market and what works. If you have a market that is in any way "green" or environmentally conscious, chances are people will think that you are just killing trees by sending out print materials. And, on top of that, it's so expensive for mailing, it may not be worthwhile.

It shocks me how many people come to me for coaching and the first thing they want to know is what to put on their one sheet. I always ask, "Why do you need a one sheet?" Typically, someone told them that they needed it, so they spend time and money developing it, only to find out that their website can work much more effectively in today's market.

ONE SHEETS *(If You Must)*

If you must have a one sheet … it should present an image to the client, give them some information about you and establish your area of expertise.

Your one sheet should say something about who you are and should immediately show the reader what it is you do, how you do it, and the value to them. The components of a one sheet are similar to that of the home page of your website and you might include some program titles and offerings.

If you are talking to a client by phone and he or she asks you to send something and you don't have a website yet, by all means send your one sheet. If you do have a website, there is no reason to be sending one sheet PDFs as a first impression piece. Send them a link to your website.

Remember that all of your materials should have the same look and feel — keep your brand consistent on your website, print materials, and video.

Demo Video

Unlike websites and print materials that are mostly for image, the main use of your demo video is to secure bookings. It should demonstrate enough of your live speaking presentation to answer the question: "Why should I hire this speaker over all of the others?" (See 2.0 update below.)

I believe that once you surpass $3,500 in your fees, the video becomes the primary decision-making tool the meeting planner will use. Picture a boardroom table with ten people sitting around it, viewing one video after another. They might be passing around your print materials at the time of viewing. They might have your website on the screen in front of them. Chances are that the way they react to the video will ultimately be the deciding factor in whether they book you or another speaker. So let's build a video that *gets you that booking*!

When you are a known expert, you get into the boardroom situation less and less. One person decides that the company needs your services (hopefully the CEO of the company) and they hire you without considering other speakers. This is when you have moved from being a commodity speaker to an expert. This is the goal. Either way, the client will want to see that you can hold your own on the platform and a killer video will help close the deal.

2.0 VIDEOS

Although we're still going to show you how to develop a demo video, the use of demos is becoming less and less necessary with the You-Tube generation. So what's the hottest way to get booked using video today? My recommendation is that you place a series of short (two to three minutes) videos on your website. There's no longer the expense of producing a demo video, nor the cost of producing an actual DVD. Save the trees (no more one sheets)! Save the DVDs!

2.0 HOME PAGE VIDEO

When someone wants to hire you to speak, they want to see you in action — first and foremost!

Many executives or planners searching for a speaker are doing web searches. That means that if they don't see what they want within the first few minutes on your home page, you may lose them. The best way to capture their attention so they'll look around is with a home page video. Again, it's short, two or three minutes max, and it's not you talking to the camera about how to use your website. It's you speaking live (ideal) or talking about the work that you do (and the benefits to others). When someone wants to hire you to speak, they want to see you in action — first and foremost!

Once you have your best video on your home page, then you may want to add more clips to the inside of your website, perhaps on the Keynotes and Workshops page. For you to outline a speech and then show an example of that presentation via video is way cool. You might have a few short videos and then, for those who really want to see more, have something that shows 20-30 minutes live.

2.0 YOUTUBE CHANNEL

YouTube and Vimeo have become great ways to attract new business, therefore, many speakers are developing a large variety of video content on their own "channel." It's a great and easy way to get your content out there and I understand that it helps raise your search rankings. Does that mean you need to run out and film a bunch of clips? No, but you can be thinking about taking a combination of live clips, along with clips of you talking one-on-one to the camera and starting your own Channel.

WHAT DOES A KILLER DEMO VIDEO LOOK LIKE?

Again, this may not be necessary, but if you really want to deliver a demo, here are the components to a successful video. The most important are discussed below.

- **Humor** — If you can make your viewing audience laugh within the first few seconds of your video, then your chances of getting booked go up. Let's go back to the scenario of a group of people watching a stack of videos. Once everyone has laughed, the energy in the room changes and they relate that good feeling back to you. If you have humor in your speech, then use it, and use it up front. Don't be afraid to put your best stuff in the demo.

- **Energy** — The toughest thing to capture on film is what happened in the room on the day you shot your video. Audience reaction is key to getting good footage. You need at least a two-camera shoot to capture the audience's reaction. Ideally you want audience members laughing, crying, being engaged, or taking notes. Capturing them laughing or clapping is a must, so make sure they are mic'd for sound.

- **Quality** — Before YouTube made three-minute videos so popular, the quality of the shoot was extremely important. Unless your brother-in-law is an experienced videographer, do not ask him to film your demo video on your family camcorder. The professionals know what they are doing. Camera angles are important, sound is important, even panning the audience takes technique. A homemade video looks like a homemade video. If you are after a quality demo, you need a quality shoot, done on quality equipment, by professionals.

- **Audience** — Consider the type of audiences that you desire (500 people or 50 people) and then try to film that same type of venue. If you seek to speak to groups of 100 or more, yet have footage of 20 people on your video, you are shooting yourself in the foot (no pun intended).

- **Patience** — No video is better than a bad video. Wait for the right opportunity to film. You need to be prepared to update your video every 12 to 18 months, so know that your first video will not be your last. You don't want to spend a fortune. Your speech is going to change, evolve, and hopefully continue to get better over time and you always want to be prepared to have your video reflect that development. If you have been speaking a short while — *Wait*. Allow your speech to evolve for two years before going down the demo video path. You can be taping yourself (either audio or video) in order to improve the speech, but don't rush the demo video.

  When I arrived at Vince Poscente's office he had already started sending out a bad demo video to bureaus and clients. It took us years to undo the damage and start working with the bureaus and clients who had viewed that video. We also made the mistake of not putting his best stuff first. We thought it was so unusual that it would scare people. That decision was based on fear. As soon as we changed it, the bookings rolled in. See Vince's flashpoint in Phase I for more on this technique.

- **Crap Shoot** — It's almost always the most amazing presentations that you don't film — ask any speaker. It's a gamble. Make it a habit to ask clients if they would like to tape your presentation for their internal use. They often respond positively. You might even encourage it in your speaker agreement. You would just ask for a high quality (digital) copy of the master in return for allowing them to film you. If they decide to do a one camera shoot, you may decide to pay for the second camera yourself. Larger conventions will often use a production company to handle all of the audio/video needs. Working with that same company can help make the filming of your presentation more seamless.

It is wise to have your expectations in writing, so that you get what you want in your video footage. That way if the filming does not turn out, you have some recourse. They may do everything right and the footage still isn't satisfactory — you may have to try more than once to get great footage.

- **Brief** — Overall, it's my opinion that a 7-10-minute video is plenty. If I'm not sold in the first 90 seconds of your video, chances are good that I won't be sold in the 22nd minute either. That being said, I have heard speakers' bureaus and meeting planners say that they prefer a full-length tape. You should have both available — a full, unedited presentation and a demo video.

  If I'm not sold in the first 90 seconds of your video, chances are good that I won't be sold in the 22nd minute either.

  A speakers' bureau owner told me about viewing videos with a CEO client one day. He put in a video, the client watched one minute and then said, "Next." They went through five videos in under ten minutes. At the end, the CEO said, "I'll take that third speaker." The client knew what he wanted and he wasn't wasting any time making a decision.

- **Expertise** — Your video must demonstrate the fact that you are credible to deliver this message. It answers "Why should I listen to you." Some people establish credibility with the use of voice-over or some sort of written commentary that tells people about you. Avoid cliché terms and anything that looks cheesy. If you have TV footage of you being interviewed, you may want to include brief clips to add to the credibility factor and the personal touch. I love one-on-one video where the speaker is talking about their brand and how it helps people. You can also include some personal elements here.

- **Style** — What the meeting planner really wants to see is you speaking — your on-stage style. There should not be five minutes of preamble before they see you speaking. Have your speaking clips available fairly close to the start of the video.

- **Answers the Question** — The bottom line is that your video answer the question, "Why should I hire this speaker?" Make sure that you do a trial run of your video on two or three clients or speakers' bureaus *before* the final edit to see if that question is being answered positively.

⚡ FLASHPOINT: Somer McCormick, former VP of Everything, Amanda Gore

Even though we didn't have a super-fancy/expensive demo, the video really sold Amanda because of the quality of the presentation captured on it. Our demo was just a free master copy we received when we allowed a client to film for archival purposes. They had a great AV team that really helped the quality, so there really wasn't any editing we had to do except top and tail it. We used this demo for years!

Tips from the Masters: *ROBIN CREASMAN*

How to Produce a First-Class Speaker Video that Rocks!

They say you can't judge a book by its cover but most of us judge people by the way they talk, the way they dress, what they say, and how they say it. We form opinions about people the first time we see or hear them. We even form opinions about people we've never met!

Think about it! Speakers' bureaus and meeting planners do the same thing. They make a judgment about you based on one item ... your demo video. It's a known fact that the single most important marketing tool for getting you booked as a professional speaker is your video. This single tool can make or break you when it comes to being reviewed by those who make the decision to hire speakers. Make a great first impression and you're good to go. Make a bad one and, well ...

There are plenty of stories of well-known and highly regarded celebrities, authors and "experts" whose video *un-sold* them to the meeting planner. Their credibility was lost because of a bad video ... be it from poor production, weak content, or lackluster presentation skills. The results were the same — *no booking!* With a good video, you can quickly rise to the top of your niche market; you can increase your fee; and you can become the talk of the industry within a very short time. Word gets around quickly with bureaus and meeting planners whether it's good or bad. Hopefully the word on you is good!

The following tips should help you on your journey to producing a "First-Class Speaker Video that Rocks!"

- **Understand Your Audience** — Understand the mind-set of the meeting planner. Like all of us, meeting planners are overworked and overwhelmed. It's not uncommon for a meeting planner to view 100 videos to book just 20 speakers for their event (five videos per speaking slot). They want a speaker who will excite and engage their attendees; one who is entertaining, insightful, humorous, and motivational; and bottom line, one who delivers a content-rich presentation with enthusiasm. So they're looking for a video that quickly grabs their attention, one that is unique and stands out from the crowd and one that captures the essence of the speaker doing what he or she does best ... speaking.

- **A First Impression Happens Only Once** — Don't blow it. Your first goal with your speaker video is to get into what I call the "maybe" pile. This is the group of videos that make it past the "trash" pile and into the "maybe" pile to be viewed again later for much more detail. *The first two minutes of your video need to rock!* Without question, this is the most important part of your video. If you waste any time with unnecessary baloney, such as the announcer with the voice of God talking about how great you are or you talking straight to the camera introducing yourself to the viewer and describing what is to come on the video or 45 seconds of fancy graphics, testimonials, and sound effects all building up to your spinning logo, then it will all be worthless and you'll be certain to make it into the "trash" pile. The first two minutes need to be great. Include short clips of you doing your best material. Mix it up with some humor, poignant sound bites, engaging moments and exciting audience reactions. Coupling this with high quality graphics and compelling music should move you to the top of the heap and into the "maybe" pile.

- **Be Good. Really, Really Good** — This may sound trite, but it is important. Many times speakers have not put their presentation under the magnifying glass and taken a hard look at what they are saying and how they are saying it. As a producer/director/editor, I'm constantly writing and rewriting the story in order to deliver it in the best possible light. When I produce speaker videos, many times I end up editing the speakers' stories to where they are better than the original. Some of the speakers say, "Wow, I didn't know I was that good." I challenge them to go and edit and rewrite their presentation so they can be as good as their demo. So it's always better to be really good before you shoot your speech. It will make your speaker video that much better.

- **Work with a Performance Coach Before You Shoot Your Presentation** — Many of you are thinking that this doesn't apply to you. If you're thinking that, chances are you could use a coach. Every speaker worth his or her salt can benefit greatly by getting professional coaching on presentation and performance skills. Why many speakers don't think they need this boggles my mind. Every successful actor, musician, athlete, or CEO has had some kind of specialized training to get him or her to the top of the field. And many continue to get coaching even when they're at the top. You may offer expert advice on a topic, you may even have written the defining, best-selling book, but that doesn't mean you are a great presenter. Great presenters have great coaches.

- **Video Tape Multiple Presentations** — Videotape as many presentations as possible. You often don't discover until it's too late that the stage and room set-up would be so professional looking or that the audience would be so responsive.

And even if you bomb you can always learn from studying yourself on tape. Moreover, when producing your demo video, you only need to excerpt small segments of great content and those segments don't all have to come from one location. As a matter of fact, multiple presentations give a more polished look to the video. They provide credibility, by showing you speaking to different groups at different times. So hire a professional crew and press record whenever possible.

- **Use Production Companies and Videographers who Know the Speaking Business** — This is very important. There are a great number of really good videographers who will say they are capable of shooting your live speech. Beware. Shooting a live speaker event needs special attention and most camera operators don't capture the experience properly without a "director" calling the shots for them. Camera placement, speaker framing, audience shots, audio configurations, etc. — all are important decisions that must be made by an experienced source. "Live" means you only have one take. There are no second chances in a live production. Most videographers don't work in a "live" situation and are not aware of the many potential problems … until it's too late. Also, ask the camera operator if they edit as well as shoot. If they don't, don't use them. Only someone who shoots and edits can fully understand how to shoot an event without the guidance of a director. A quick note about rates for professional videographers: the national average for a "one-man band" videographer (one DVCam, Beta SP or DV video camera, wireless audio setup, and a small three-light lighting kit) runs about $1000–$1200. A two-operator, two-camera package would run about $1650–$2000. Some video crews offer full-day rates and half-day rates. If you book a crew at a half-day rate for five hours and you roll over into six, you are automatically billed the full-day rate. Full days typically start at first crew call of the assignment and end when the assignment is wrapped, even if small breaks or lunch were taken in between.

  Your producer or editor must understand the industry in order to capture the most important features of a great speaker video. Choose your production company wisely. This is not the time to try out cousin Celia's husband who dabbles in video editing.

- **A Two-Camera Shoot is Better than One, but Three is Best** — A two-camera shoot is always better than a single camera. Having two different angles to cut between is a huge plus when it comes to editing the video. You can set this up in one of two ways. The most obvious approach is to hire two people to shoot two cameras. Camera 1 follows the speaker framed "feet or waist up" and never loses site of the speaker. Camera 2 moves around the room shooting the speaker from different angles and capturing a variety of crowd shots or B-Roll.

- **Dress Out the Stage for a Bigger Look: Think Big** — This is a real problem most speakers come up against at one time or another. The staging for most events is the standard hotel ballroom or meeting room with a small stage positioned against a wall. Many times the stage is blocking a doorway with an exit sign appearing right behind the speaker. Sometimes there is not a stage, but just a small area at the front where the speaker is to stand. At other times, a podium is positioned right in the middle of the presentation area. These scenarios are all very common. The best situation is to have as large a stage as possible with "Pipe and Drape" used for the background. This is something that all hotels can provide. You've seen this — the black or blue curtains that stand behind the stage. This offers a professional look and can be enhanced with a variety of props, special lighting, plants, scrims, video screens, etc., to make your event appear larger and more professional. Talk with the meeting planner a few weeks ahead of time and see if they can provide any of this for you. If they don't want to pay the associated fees, see if they will split the expense or, as a last resort, pay for it yourself. Typical cost for pipe and drape with plants shouldn't run more than $400–$500. Definitely worth the expense for your video shoot.

- **Open Strong ... Finish Great** — In the world of entertainment production, "beginnings and endings" are the most important part of any production. At the beginning of a television show, you are competing with many other options ... 200 other channels, the Internet, family commitments, hobbies, personal agendas, reading, or whatever. Again, the first two minutes have to "hook" the viewer or the viewer will change the channel. The same is true in a live event. You have two minutes to capture the attention of the audience or *they will tune you out*. If you come on stage and talk about how good it is to be there or how difficult your flight was or something unrelated to your message, then you're missing your best opportunity to gain audience buy-in. That theory translates to your video too: the first two minutes need to Rock!

Master Robin Creasman, *President of Robin Creasman Productions, is an award-winning television producer and director and has over 20 years of experience in the entertainment, music and speaking industry.*

The next phase in the Wealthy Speaker Process is to roll-out to your market. If you've gotten ready, taken aim, then you're ready to fire.

5

Phase III
FIRE

Rolling Out to Your Market

· ·

If you think making your speech great, positioning yourself as an expert and developing the appropriate marketing materials was tough, you need to take a deep breath. You've only just started. Now you need to identify your target market and determine the best method to reach them. You need to roll out your product and continue to build momentum. You're *ready*, you've taken *aim*, now *fire*!

 ### ROLL OUT

You've probably had your audience type in mind all along, otherwise it would have been difficult to write the copy for your website. When we talk target markets, we're taking that one step further. We might focus on specific industries where your audience decision makers would be.

An example might be that you want to offer a leadership talk. You write your site with leaders in mind. But when it comes to reaching out to them, where do you go? Well, this is where we break it down and try some testing in different industries. Perhaps you target leaders in insurance, financial, and real estate to start. That's where you'll focus your outbound efforts.

Public Relations (PR): Fire Your Message to the Masses

There are a number of ways to get your message out. It all comes down to selling yourself — or at least your expertise. Many people start their roll out with a book launch and that includes PR, so we've placed it here first. If that's not the case for you, you might try some of the other roll out techiques before tackling the press. Some speakers don't put a PR plan into place at all, and that's okay. Just skim this section for now and come back to it when needed. Or, pick out a few ideas and begin a "PR Campaign Lite."

 COACH'S QUESTION: *What methods have you used to get your name, message and expertise out to your target market and potential audiences?*

If you've been letting the local media know that you are presenting a speech at the local merchant's group — good for you. If you've written a press release about the decline in sales in downtown shops due to the big box mall on the edge of town — better for you. If you've been submitting a monthly column in the local paper about retailing — best for you. Whether it be writing articles for your industry magazine or getting a slot on CNN, getting press can help set you up as the expert.

APPROACHING THE PRESS

Be very focused about getting press before you start your campaign. Some speakers will tell you that a cross-country book tour did not garner any speaking engagements. Perhaps being on the radio or TV during the middle of the day meant that their entire target market was at work while they were being interviewed.

Think of your marketing campaign before taking action. Here are a few questions to ask yourself.

1. Will getting PR in the medium I am considering establish me as an expert in my field?
2. Will it get noticed by my target market?
3. Can I use it to add to my credibility?
4. Will it ultimately help me move toward my speaking goals?

There are many excellent books on getting good PR and many excellent coaches in the field. One of the main reasons speakers would use a PR firm is to promote a book they would like to make a bestseller. For the most part, huge amounts of time, energy, and money go into promoting bestselling books. Ask someone like Jack Canfield, co-author of the "Chicken Soup" series. When they first started out, no publisher would even talk to them. Once they did have a deal, they did tremendous amounts of press, many days getting up at 4:00 A.M. for radio interviews.

Occasionally, press can be a huge career booster — as in the case of motivational speaker Keith Harrell. Keith's speech on attitude had developed such a following that the *Wall Street Journal* did a full-page story on him. The article was every speaker's dream come true. Keith's fee jumped substantially in the years following that article.

Press can also have minimal impact. Several years ago, I secured a cover story in the local business magazine for the speaker I represented. I thought, "This is it! We've made it! We've busted through!" Not true. It probably secured us two or three local engagements and that was it. However, we inserted a color copy of that cover in every speaking packet that went out the door from then on, so it did lend credibility, even if it didn't make our business.

Make sure you are clear on the angle of the story and be very careful before agreeing to an interview. You might just be made out to be a buffoon.

And, as we all know, press can have a negative impact. Years ago a motivational speaker was written up negatively in *Fortune* magazine and he was absolutely devastated by it. The press may not see the value of what professional speakers do, so tread softly if they approach you about doing a story about speakers. Make sure you are clear on the angle of the story and be very careful before agreeing to an interview. You might just be made out to be a buffoon.

That being said, if you do get negative press, don't let it tank your career. Focus on the value that you give to your audiences to boost yourself.

PRESS RELEASES

The mistake that I see most speakers making is sending out a press release that does not answer the question: "So what"? They don't tie it to anything relevant into which the press can sink their teeth.

One of my clients was putting on a seminar for business owners, so he drafted up a press release stating the details of the seminar with times and dates. Once we talked about the "so what" factor, he changed it to add a very forceful headline, "80% of Businesses Are Designed to Fail," and went on to give reasons why and what they needed to do to avoid failure. Now his seminar looked more attractive and the press release added value for the reader. Some of the local press picked it up and helped sell more seats to the seminar.

Have a very clear goal in mind when you start a press release and then work backwards thinking about how you can provide value to the press. They need to provide solid content for their readers or viewers and you have content to provide.

BEING THE EXPERT IN THE PRESS

Rather than approaching the press to sell them on an idea, approach them with the idea that you are the expert with something to offer them. Many talk radio stations and breakfast TV shows are looking for content of interest to their viewers. It's helpful to know what demographic or market each station goes after before you approach them.

The key is your hook and finding a way to get yourself noticed in the pile of press releases. There are some basic techniques for approaching the press.

1. Have a hook — something that will catch their attention.
2. Make it timely — see what else is going on in the news and if you can piggyback on another story or issue.
3. Be very clear about which issue you are addressing — you are an expert on selling to women, so the headline that you

piggyback might read "75% of all buying decisions are made by women" or "salesmen are missing the mark." You might then offer "Ten tips to help men sell to women."

TRADE MAGAZINES AND BLOGS

Ideally, in order to establish yourself as an expert in your industry or niche, you'll want to publish articles in the appropriate trade journals and blogs. Many publications are open to taking content from outside sources. The ideal time to approach a magazine is after you've spoken to a group; however, it can often be a way to get your foot in the door for a speaking engagement. Be sure to read the magazine or blog first to make sure you know the audience. You may also choose to customize an existing article for each target market and offer it up for submission. It will take time to become known with the magazines, but if you are consistent about keeping in touch, it will pay off.

I can't think of anyone who has leveraged media better than speaker and author Jeffrey Gitomer. He has a sales column in almost every business journal in the U.S. Between his books *The Sales Bible* and *Little Red Book of Selling* and his column, he is well known as *the* guy to go to for sales. What better way to make yourself a business household name? When someone reads your column each week, they get to know you personally and become a follower or part of your choir. When Jeffrey runs public seminars, it's a no brainer that his readership will attend — and, of course, buy scads of his products. They've become old friends!

EXPERT AVAILABLE FOR COMMENT

Journalists go to online services when they are seeking experts on particular topics. You might consider getting yourself listed with some of these services so that you can be found when they need you.

2.0 PR WIRE SERVICES

There's a service called HARO.com — Help a Reporter Out — that you can sign up for and receive notices from journalists who are seeking experts on particular topics. You'll have to dig a bit, but it could really pay off.

There are also services popping up daily that allow your articles to go out on a PR Wire or service. At the time of writing this book, some examples are: newswire.ca, prweb.com, prnewsire.com, just to name a few.

When I asked my PR Firm, EMSI, how they generated so much activity for the Frog book we were promoting (the PR was a huge success, but the book sales were not), they provided the following analysis:

> *A lot of really big stuff we got for your campaign actually wasn't from using a wire service. The campaigns are way more involved and require a lot more work than just distributing a piece on a wire service. The big hits we got for you (Huffington Post, Yahoo! Shine, BeliefNet, YourTango, etc.) were from working directly with our contacts in the media.*
>
> *The wire service we do use, though, is: www.marketwire.com/.*

> **WEBSITE REFERENCE TOOL**
>
> **www.speakerlauncher.com** ➡
> **Book Buyer LOGIN** *(red button)*
> **Check Out:** *www.marketwire.com,*
> *www.newswire.ca, www.prweb.com,*
> and *www.prnewswire.com.*

HIRING AN AGENCY OR PUBLICIST

Self-promotion is not easy for most people and it is a full-time job in and of itself. Hiring an agency or publicist can lighten your load. Some of the things you'll want to consider before hiring someone to help you promote yourself or your book are listed below. You could also use this list when researching a PR agency.

1. Do they know my market?
2. Do they understand my goals?
3. Do they have the contacts that I need?
4. Do they have a good reputation?
5. What is their track record?

6. Will they work hard for me or will I get lost in the pile?

7. Who has used them with success? Try to find some of your own references as well as the ones they provide. Ask them for at least six people, then call the bottom of the list first.

8. If possible, go to their offices and see how organized they are — if it's mayhem, then you may reconsider.

9. Will I have to sign a long-term contract? If so, then think very carefully. Many speakers have been completely dissatisfied with their PR firms, so make sure you have a trial period before locking into anything long term. Or better yet, use an agency on a project basis.

Not all PR agents are going to have wins every single time. Know your odds and exactly what activities your dollars are going towards. If the cost of your agency is so high that you have to mortgage your home, then don't do it. There are too many companies out there to choose from to take on more financial burden than you can handle.

2.0 PR AGENCIES

Always bring the costs of your PR agency back to something tangible. For example: I only have to book two speeches for this entire campaign to pay for itself. If you're goal is strickly to sell books, you may have to evaluate your costs closely.

When launching *The Frog Whisperer*, I was offered a campaign for $1500 to book 10 radio shows. Although this amount didn't break the bank, I didn't take the campaign. Why? Because those shows may not have been specific enough for my market and I would not have sold the 150 books I needed to break even. I decided instead to market directly to radio shows that were dating and advice shows — much more targeted.

When I reviewed the costs of using my PR agency for the Frog campaign, it did not pay off in book sales, despite what we all considered a really great response.

Finding Business

Do you believe that your business doesn't need to be a struggle? Can you wrap your mind around the idea that if you get very clear on what you want, you can make it happen? Olympic athletes are very good at using their mind to achieve what they want. Because I spent four years working with a former Olympian, I believe wholeheartedly in the power of the mind.

THE ATTRACTION METHOD

Now I know this sounds a little odd to most people, but if you'll just give the process a chance you may be surprised. The book that I recommend to all of my clients on this topic is called *Attracting Perfect Customers: The Power of Strategic Synchronicity* by Stacy Hall and Jan Brogniez. It leads you through a four-step process to attracting the customers that you desire. I won't go into the entire book, but the first step is getting very clear on identifying your perfect customer. I would break that down even further to define who your perfect audience is as well. If you are just starting out in the speaking industry, you will need to go out and speak a lot before you will really know who is perfect for you. You might have to do a lot of speaking engagements that are not right for you, before you can see clearly who is the best, most perfect audience.

WEBSITE REFERENCE TOOL

www.speakerlauncher.com ➡ Book Buyer LOGIN *(red button)*

Recommended Reading: *Attracting Perfect Customers: The Power of Strategic Synchronicity* by Stacy Hall and Jan Brogniez.

Once you are clear, you can start drafting a list of the qualities of your perfect customer. As a coach, some of the traits of my perfect customers are as follows: they show up on time and are eager and ready to grow; they are coachable; they want to hear the truth; they pay on time, gladly, and can easily afford my services. In order to develop the profile of your perfect customer, try Coaching Exercise 10.

As a speaker, your list might look something like this: they see me as *the* expert and trust me; I am the only choice; therefore price is not an issue; they treat me with respect and do everything they can to help make my program a success; they are enjoyable to work with; they pay gladly and on time; and they send me three referrals.

One of the steps in the attraction model is realizing what you need to improve in order to attract your perfect customers. One major step for new speakers is working on the speech. The attraction process will only work if the speech (your product) is ready for the audience that you desire. In order to balance the attraction process, you need to ensure that you can manage the level of business that you want to attract.

In order to balance the attraction process, you need to ensure that you can manage the level of business that you want to attract.

Coaching Exercise 10: QUALITIES OF YOUR PERFECT CUSTOMER

The first step is getting very clear on identifying your perfect customer. If you are just starting out in the speaking industry, you will need to go out and speak a lot before you will really know who is perfect for you. You might have to do a lot of speaking engagements that are not right for you, before you can see clearly who is the best, most perfect audience.

Your Perfect Customer: Sample

You've been speaking professionally for six months and have been told by several people that you are really good. So you start to draft your perfect customer list. You write that your perfect client has audiences of more than 5,000 people and they are all CEOs.

If in your seventh month of speaking, you speak to this audience, you could be making a huge career blunder. The reason? Unless you are freakishly talented, the odds are that you aren't ready for this group. It may take two or three years to be able to handle a group of that size and stature and it's important that you ensure you are ready before you get in front of them. You might start with groups of 50–100 CEOs and work your way up.

Your Perfect Customer

List the qualities of your perfect customer (including what their audience might look like).

1. _____

2. _____

3. _____

4. _____

5. _____

6. _____

I would highly recommend walking through all of the steps in the book *Attracting Your Perfect Customer.*

You can also find all of these exercises in a separate and conveniently bound workbook: *Wealthy Speaker Workbook and Planning Guide.*

NICHE MARKETING

One of the major benefits of having a niche is it gives you focus. Niche marketing allows you to develop a strong presence within a field. Your niche markets will most likely become your target market. Then when you launch, or relaunch, yourself, you know exactly where to start and who to contact. Without a niche, you're just throwing darts to see what sticks. That may be okay for a short while, but it's not very strategic.

Let's say you want to speak on sales and you want to specialize in the pharmaceutical industry. That helps you have more clarity when reaching out with your marketing, yes?

When searching out your niche, think back on your career and see where there might be opportunities for you to speak.

I had a client last year who came out of the call center industry. He had worked his way up to managing call centers at a very young age and had some outstanding results in the recent years. He was known as a leader in the call center community. When we first started talking, he wanted to speak on leadership to the corporate world. As we continued to dig, however, it made more sense to be a big fish in the call center pond, than to be one of thousands of leadership speakers in the larger corporate ocean.

Take Your Background into Account

If you are having a hard time finding a niche, then take a look back over the last 20 groups to whom you have spoken. Start analyzing them through new eyes and ask some questions.

- Which of these groups did I love?
- Which of these groups loved me?
- Who did I impact the most?
- Who can I help most in the future?
- Which of the groups could afford me without struggle?
- Which groups hold the most opportunity for future speaking engagements?

Finding your niche can sometimes take months or even years. Many speakers work for every group in every industry and that is perfectly acceptable. Often they will have moved in and around companies and industries simply because word of mouth spreads.

When you are starting an outbound marketing campaign, it's best to have a niche in mind before rolling it out. Again, focus is king!

Positioning Within Your Niche

I said it earlier, in Phase I: Ready, but it bears repeating: positioning is everything. How are you thought of within your niche? Do they know you as someone who is always trying to sell yourself to them or do people know you as *the* expert, as *the* only choice? When you are positioned as the expert, fees become much less of an issue.

Elizabeth is a sales speaker in the retail industry. She competes with other sales speakers for client budgets. Elizabeth decides to narrow her focus and become a closing expert. She writes a book, gets a great publisher, and begins a column in the retail journals on closing skills. Now when retailers call Elizabeth to come and speak on closing skills, she is the only choice in their minds. And bonus, her closing ratios have gone through the roof, so she's become even more congruent with her message.

Your mission:
*Be the **only** choice*
for your clients!

INNER CIRCLE

When getting ready to launch a new business, or a new direction in an existing business, many people forget to explore their backyard. Who is your inner circle? Your core group of supporters or choir? They will include past colleagues and employers, past clients, friends, family, neighbors, etc.

The reaction of your choir to anything new that you are promoting should be your litmus test — the gauge by which you measure the potential of new ideas. Now, don't get me wrong, I'm not saying you should ask for everyone's approval or a consensus before moving forward — we know it's impossible to please everyone. This is a way to find out if your past clients would buy what you are selling. If they say no then you have to go back to the drawing board. Asking your past clients to beta test a new keynote or workshop is a great way to get them on board with it, fine tune the program, possibly film it (if it's ready) and get some testimonials about the results of the program. The testing process might look something like what is outlined below.

- Put new program/keynote/workshop together.
- Develop a marketing draft, web page or one sheet* of the idea and the benefits.
- Run it up the flagpole with your choir — a short e-mail is usually effective.
- Ask past clients to hold an event so that you can deliver this new program.
- Film the event, if the program is solid. (As noted in Phase II: Aim, always wait until your program has a solid delivery before capturing it on video. Jumping the gun on filming yourself is a waste of time and money.)
- Ask for testimonials — what changed as a result of your program.
- Gauge the results and tweak if necessary.
- If successful, roll it out to your target market.

2.0 NICHE MARKETING

One of my clients was a general business expert. He worked in and around the corporate world for ten years before stumbling into the niche market of health care. What we determined was that health care understood the concepts best and were in huge need of his services. Sometimes we fall into our niche, and sometimes we choose it strategically. Either way, it helps to have this focus.

---

* See Phase II: Aim for an update on the use of one sheets.

SPEAK WHEREVER THEY WILL LISTEN

When you are in the building stages of your career, you may need to spend a number of months doing free engagements (see Figure H: Orbits of the Speaking World). For a short period of time, you may decide to speak to any group who will provide an audience. That might include all of your local networking groups, Toastmasters, Rotary Clubs, Chambers of Commerce, etc. From all of these events — perhaps you do freebies for a period of six months — you should have a fairly nice stack of leads for prospective business. If each presentation doesn't garner some interest for more business, then you must continue to work on the presentation.

You may decide to speak to any group who will provide an audience.

Aside from these freebies turning into some paid engagements, you'll also want to use this opportunity to build a database. See Building a Database later in this chapter to make sure you are taking full advantage of every speaking engagement.

RUNNING YOUR OWN SHOWCASE

When I was working with leadership expert Betska K-Burr, we decided to put together a showcase in our hometown of London,

Ontario, to help her gain more local recognition as an expert. We had made some inroads in our own backyard, but we really needed to build momentum.

I asked the local radio station with our demographic to get involved. We offered them free admission for their staff and gave them a number of tickets to hand out to their clients. In turn they gave us some free radio spots. We charged a small amount to attend and, as soon as the radio announcements kicked in, the phone was ringing with registrations. We also partnered with our local business magazine and had them advertise (quarter page ad) for us in lieu of a sponsorship package that included some free seats, etc. They gave away a trial subscription at the event. All of our partners had their materials on hand and were allowed to put up banners and speak for three minutes each, before Betska spoke.

We invited the press to come free of charge and our local clients and prospects were also given complimentary seats. We arranged barter with the hotel and AV company — allowing their clients and staff to come for free. So our out-of-pocket expenses were handouts and we provided the coffee and tea. That was it. We filled a good size meeting room with about 150 people and everyone loved the event — and Betska. We closed several pieces of business later that week and got the momentum that we desired. I don't recall if it was a direct result of that event, but later that year Betska got the cover story in the local business magazine. Think about how you can run showcases for your clients or the press and get your sponsors to help fill the room for you! Many of the same principles could apply — finding sponsors, trading advertising for tickets, etc. — for running your own public seminars.

Rolling Out to Your Market

Now you come to the nitty-gritty. It's time to put everything together and book those engagements. You'll need to get your attitude set, decide who to call, be creative, and follow through.

HOW TO BOOK A GIG

When starting out, you'll need to make a lot of calls and follow up in a consistent manner. A great method is call-send-call. It will be tempting to contact a speakers' bureau — after all, they are the people who book speakers. Resist the temptation.

First of all, you need to go through the process of contacting prospects yourself. Those initial conversations and follow-up calls will help you hone your client conversations. The value of this feedback and practical experience cannot be overrated.

Once you have a few years' experience and 30 or more paid speeches per year at a decent fee under your belt, you might be ready to approach a speakers' bureau. Speakers' bureaus are an entity unto themselves and you will likely want to run through a ready, aim, fire process just for them. So leave them off your list for a couple of years and when you're ready, turn to Chapter 6.

2.0 CALL-SEND-CALL

Remember that building the relationship is the goal and it doesn't matter how you go about doing it.

In today's climate, the phone might be considered a bit out of date. Shooting off a query e-mail will probably be the more likely procedure. Just remember that building the relationship is the goal and it doesn't matter how you go about doing it. Joe Calloway doesn't hesitate to hop on a plane if a client wants to discuss doing some work with him. A face-to-face sales call might be considered kind of old school, but guess what? It works! We can't forget the basics of developing relationships.

Call-Send-Call — The Process

When I first started in the business, roughly 20 years ago, the call-send-call method was the primary way of getting booked into speeches. I learned this technique from Thom Winninger. You'd call someone to establish a need, send materials, and then call back. It was effective! I think for the most part it will always work, but the way the client makes the decision will continue to become more sophisticated. There is a basic seven-step process that outlines the call-send-call method.

1. Identify the prospect.

2. Call or e-mail them and find out when they are planning for their next event.

3. Establish that you speak on a topic that may be of interest to that group.

4. Establish that they can afford you.

5. When they are in the planning stages, provide them with your materials via your website. Ask them what they need to see to make their decision. They may require that you show them some video. They may say that they'll watch your video online and print pages from your website. Sometimes they have to pass your materials around or send them to a meeting. So it's important that you have what they need available.

6. Find out when the decision will be finalized.

7. Follow up at the appropriate time.

If there is some lag time during this process, you might send them a current article or testimonials to keep your name top of mind. Try to remind them about yourself without stalking them.

But before you ever pick up the phone or send the e-mail, you want to get clear on your value and make sure that you have the right approach. You also want to research as much as you can about their event. If the information is readily available on their website, don't waste their time asking the (where and when is your next meeting) questions.

YOUR APPROACH

Bringing Value to an Organization

When you are first starting out in the industry you will most likely be thinking about booking one speech at a time. You're really finding your way in the industry and you have to start somewhere. However, if you can take a broader approach from the beginning and think about the question, "How can I bring *value* to this organization?" then you'll be on the right track. Although the techniques outlined are designed to book "a speech," always be thinking big picture with a company.

Are You Being the Lighthouse?

In the book *Attracting Your Perfect Customer: The Power of Strategic Synchronicity*, the authors talk about expertise being your lighthouse. You stand tall on the shore offering up your expertise to ships (clients) who need help getting to shore. When a storm emerges, the ships that require your services will follow the beam. What we don't want to do is have the lighthouse sprout arms and legs and run up and down the beach saying, "Follow me, follow me!" That is not attraction; it's desperation. You need to make it easy for them to see that you have what they need and allow them to buy (vs. being sold).

Wealthy Speakers stand tall in their expertise, knowing that they have what some (not all) clients need.

Sales tools can definitely be useful when talking to a client. Knowing how to move from probing to close will help you book business more easily. Being in the mode of attraction does not mean taking no action. An essential part of the attraction process is knowing what you need to do to become more attractive to a client and being very clear on the value you bring to the table. Sometimes that means getting your act together in terms of your speech, your marketing materials or your process of moving a client through a presentation. Once you are truly ready, the door of the attraction process is fully open to you.

FLASHPOINT: Cheryl Cran, CSP

My pivotal moment or "clear" path was when I paid Alan Weiss for an hour of his time. He said a few things that shifted my thinking about the business. He told me there is no conscious barrier for women in the speaking business, but women needed to get over being liked and focus on providing value. This really resonated with me. He also went on to tell me that the only thing stopping me from being a million dollar speaker was my own limited beliefs. In order to grow I needed to dig deeper with my clients and not allow myself to do "one off" speaking engagements that are good for the ego, but not the pocketbook.

Because of Alan I shifted to selling large contracts when contacted by prospects. This was about 18 months ago. Now, when they ask me about a speaking engagement, I move the conversation toward identifying the clients' needs, their goals, hopes, and visions. What does the client want their company or group to look like in six months, one year? Once they answer those questions, I tell them that a speech is only the beginning of a powerful transformation and that together we could implement programs that would create lasting change. My business model consists of speeches that 90% of the time are followed by consulting and projects.

The result is that I have a deeper and longer lasting impact with the organization, referrals are a no-brainer, and I'm getting reference letters that speak to results, transformation, and change.

I am happier with what I am doing because it gives me great satisfaction to be able to see the difference I'm making. Also I'm enjoying the keynotes more because I'm bringing practical experience and results to them. God I love this business!

2.0 CHERYL CRAN

It's been five years since I wrote about my business in Jane's book — time goes fast when you are having fun! I am still invested in this business with heart and soul. I have worked with Jane more than once over the past five years to continue refreshing my brand. The uncertain economy has really helped me to continue to define my value proposition for clients. I've worked with different coaches and in January 2012 I worked with Alan Weiss again. Here is where I am now:

1. I am continuing to invest time in building myself as a thought leader in my area of expertise, which is leadership, generations, and technology. I have worked to hone the art

of stagecraft, deliver value for clients consistently, and build my keynote brand in North America. Alan Weiss says, "Not all consultants are great keynoters and it's rare for someone to be good at both."

2. I am refocused (for a while I got too busy and was leaving money on the table) on looking longer term with my clients. In fact I just presented two keynotes and landed two major consulting opportunities by simply having strategic discussions at the time of booking, when in front of the client, and as a follow-up practice post-keynote.

3. I believe that the future of business is about focused diversity. This means focusing on your expertise but being diverse with your delivery methods. Technology is adding to the delivery channel options we all have. When we focus on our expertise and have diverse channels of delivery we can expand our value to our clients while continually developing material and value based on our expertise.

4. The biggest change in the past five years for me is having a life. I am less intensely focused on the drive to get somewhere and instead am enjoying "being here." I meditate twice a day, I have healthy habits, and I am enjoying my life versus delaying the enjoyment. This business is fantastic. It allows us to give in a big way, get rewarded in big ways, and continually grow.

MATCHING VERSUS COLD CALLING

When you are preparing to make your phone calls or send query e-mails you want to be wearing your attraction hat rather than your sales hat. It wouldn't hurt for you to know how to sell, but, basically, when you are picking up the phone it should be to see whether or not the client has a need that your services match. That being said, get yourself into attraction or matching mode by thinking about the value that you have to offer (you are the expert) before picking up the phone. Coaching Exercise 11, The Value You Offer, can help keep you focused when making calls. Now that you are in the right mode, you're ready to start making calls.

Coaching Exercise 11: THE VALUE YOU OFFER

List the value that you bring to an organization. Organize your list and print it out in bullet form and post it in front of you before picking up the phone to make "matching" calls. Remember when you are talking to prospective clients to give them stories that they can "hang their hat on."

The Value I Offer: Sample _____

1. I provide a strategy for increasing sales.
2. My strategy covers three areas that are integral to selling success: authenticity, integrity, and value.
3. My average clients ROI is a 25% increase in customer loyalty.
4. My client, ABC company, used these techniques to close two $50,000 deals within a one-week period.

The Value I Offer _____

1. _____

    _____

    _____

2. _____

    _____

    _____

3. _____

    _____

    _____

You can also find all of these exercises in a separate and conveniently bound workbook: *Wealthy Speaker Workbook and Planning Guide.*

WHO TO CALL

Being specific about your target market or focus is always the way to go. That doesn't mean you won't try some things that will fail and then move on to new ideas, but you want to be focused in your tests. Choose a target market that matches the following criteria:

1. What industries need your message?
2. What industries can afford you?
3. What industries have enough business to keep you speaking for several years?
4. What groups of people are you passionate about and enjoy presenting to?

If you are a speaker who has a message about leadership, you may decide to define your target market as business owners. From there you would want to find associations that cater to business owners (National Association of Small Business Owners, or if you want to target women, National Association of Women Business Owners). On the other hand, you may decide that your topic is on the lighter side, like lowering stress through laughter. You could offer this up to industries that are "helping hands" types, like teachers or nurses. In this case, you might have to do some digging to discover what types of associations those people join.

You want to be doing what the competition isn't doing and there are many ways to market your business.

Why Start with Associations?

I will preface this by saying that almost every speaker has the same idea of marketing to associations, so if you know of a different path — *take it*! You want to be doing what the competition isn't doing and there are many ways to market your business.

The association market is a good starting point for many reasons.

- They are consistent — almost every association has at least one meeting or convention each year.
- It's easy to find out from their websites when the meetings are held and if they use outside speakers. This is where knowing your competition will come in handy.

- Many associations frequently hire professional speakers.

- Association audiences are full of hundreds or thousands of people from corporations. Why not speak to people from 500 different companies? The exposure couldn't be any better.

You can research nearly every type of association in the U.S. and some of Canada by going to asaenet.org and using their directory search feature. If you want to search sales associations, then just use "sales" as your search phrase and you will see a list of hundreds of sales associations and links to their websites.

> **WEBSITE REFERENCE TOOL**
>
> www.speakerlauncher.com ➡
> Book Buyer LOGIN *(red button)*
> **Check Out:** The Center for Association Leadership.

You can also buy a directory of associations for about $250. You might consider paying a little more to get your updates electronically, so that your list is as current as possible. I don't recommend one over the other. Take a look at the association directory in the library and compare it to asaenet.org before making a decision for yourself.

2.0 ASSOCIATIONS

The association market has not been immune to the economy in the past three or four years. They've taken a hit! If you can help them bring value to their members or pull in new members, then you will be valuable to them.

COLD CALLS VERSUS QUERY E-MAILS

Let's imagine that your prospective clients — association meeting planners — are getting an average of 150–200 e-mails per day. That's probably not too far from the truth. Now imagine how many meetings they have to attend and how many voice messages from speakers and speakers' bureaus they would have once they return. You can see that getting their attention is going to be a challenge, so you need to think outside of the box. Use the list of attention getters below to start your creative juices flowing.

- Call and leave an after-hours message — short, sweet, and to the point. "This is John Smith calling. I'm the author of Selling with Integrity and I'm calling about your July 20XX conference. If this topic is of interest, please check out my website at sellingwithintegrity.com and drop me a line or call (555) 555-1999."

- Offer them something for free. John Smith might have an article that the association would like to put into its newsletter.

- Send them a postcard.

- Send them a one- to two-line e-mail that asks one open-ended question, such as "When will you be planning for the July 20XX event?" It gives them an option to reply very quickly.

- Send them a bulky package (candy or something) with a thumb drive with your video.

- Try to meet them in person. Attend one of their events or offer your services to their office.

- Invite them to one of your speaking engagements.

- If you know a speaker who has already spoken to the group, ask them to put in a good word for you. *Word of mouth* is the most powerful marketing method.

- Partner with a sponsor who wants to get in front of the same groups you do. If you speak to sales audiences, you may want to partner with a company like Sage Software, which manufactures ACT! software for salespeople. Sage Software gets to be the hero by sponsoring your talk and you get to speak in front of your target audience.

COLD CALLING — QUESTIONS TO ASK

Make notes about the person in your database so you can continue the relationship every time you talk. Remember that this call is about meeting *their* needs. Don't "show up and throw up." This means don't call them and start spouting all of the great things about you as a speaker.

Your opening might be something like, "This is John Smith calling about your July 20XX event. Do you have a minute?" Once they give you the go ahead, then ask questions to establish a need. If they say "No, this isn't a good time," do your best to reschedule. You will often find that they are not the key contact. Some key questions are listed below, and note that you must be respectful of people's time. You might only get one or two questions answered when you notice that they are anxious to hang up.

*Remember that this call is about meeting **their** needs. Don't "show up and throw up."*

• • • • • • • • • • • •

- Are you the person who is in charge of booking the speakers for your upcoming conferences? If not, who?
- When is your next event?
- When will you be planning for this event? If they say six months from now, try to gain more information about the event and schedule a time to call back.
- How many paid speakers will you book for this event? "Paid" is the key word. If this association doesn't pay its speakers, then move on.
- How is the decision made? By one person? Who? By committee?
- What topics will you want to include in this year's conference? Ask if your topic would be of interest to this audience. Make sure you state the benefits of the speech.
- What is your budget for each speaker? Breakout? Keynote? Ask about your specific slot.
- In what city will the event be held? You should know this ahead of time.
- How many people will attend?
- What is the demographic? What job(s) do they do?
- What is your theme? This is your opportunity to talk about how your speech would fit. Keep asking questions about the group's needs to keep his or her interest. You may even suggest he or she go to your website while on the line with you.
- Who did you have speaking last year? Try to know this ahead of time as well and be prepared to discuss how you might follow up with that speaker.

- When will you make the decision regarding speakers?
- May I send you materials? Which format suits best — web, e-mail, mail, video, DVD, CD?
- When will you be reviewing my materials?
- When should I get back in touch? How? Phone, e-mail?

The Click — The Good Kind

Hopefully the prospect doesn't hang up on you — that would be the undesirable click. The good kind of click is when you are talking to a prospect and you feel a shift in energy when he or she becomes interested — as opposed to being polite. That is when you know you have his or her interest and can start building a relationship. If you never get the "click," then it's an uphill battle.

 COACH'S QUESTION: *What can I say to prospects on the phone that will result in gaining their interest — the "click"?*

Do your research. Bring up specific details about the company, such as what is on the website. You also need to listen carefully and respond to the needs they express. Don't forget to mention your value/benefits, but phrase it in terms of their needs. Make it about them. For instance, you might say, "Joanne, when I was studying your association's website, I noticed that you had a lot of sales training scheduled throughout the year for your people. Would a program that could help them build 25% more customer loyalty be helpful to your audience?"

The Other End of the Line

Picture the client hanging up from your conversation and picking up the phone five minutes later to have the same conversation with another speaker or bureau. You must always be aware that they may be overwhelmed by calls from people. If they are not really interested, they may use the "Can you send me some materials?" line to get you off the phone. If that happens, try to qualify a little more before hanging up. You need to be sympathetic to what they go through in a day. Try to make light of it. Ask if they have a giant hole where they throw all of the speakers' materials or talk to them about how harried their day might be. The more you can understand their position, the better you will be able to build the relationship. Remember to place notes about the conversation in your database for future reference.

Mark Levin, Executive Vice President of Chain Link Fence Manufacturers Institute, describes planning for his institute's annual meeting.

> When our association's annual meeting is coming up, we start getting intense about six months out. That's when we have to start making final decisions on programs, speakers, off-property functions, etc. Although we (as a small association) try to book speakers that are geographically close to our meeting site, it's certainly not the determining factor. In recent years we've been getting many speakers who quote us airfare-inclusive fees that make it easier to make a final decision.
>
> In general, our "outside" (outside of our specific industry) speakers are booked based on three or four key issues.
>
> 1. The right topic for our group (usually humor or personal development).
> 2. The right delivery, based on one or more criteria (in order of priority):
>   - I've seen them live.
>   - I've seen them on their website via video clip.
>   - I've seen an actual video.
>   - Someone I trust *completely* has seen and recommended them.
> 3. The right price.
> 4. How the first phone call felt? (Were they interested, responsive, and friendly; did they ask me the right questions about our group?)

SCREENING/SELECTING SPEAKERS

Mark Levin goes on to say that in today's market, there are a couple of other ways I screen/select speakers.

1. I still look at websites and website videos, but now a speaker's YouTube channel might have a wider variety of their speeches on it than just what's directly on their website. So I check that out, too.

2. Is sponsorship a possibility? Does the speaker have corporate sponsors that I can contact or does the speaker have something I might be able to present to my larger corporate members?

Like everything else, timing is key. If the speaker contacts me during that decision-making period and getting to see the speaker in action is easy and quick, there is a good chance I'll make a decision quickly. Meeting planners are looking for any reason to put you in the "yes" or "no" pile just so that they can make a decision.

> *Meeting planners are looking for any reason to put you in the "yes" or "no" pile just so that they can make a decision.*

The Simple Things Get You in the Door

Surprisingly enough, I've started many conversations with the weather. Living in a place like Canada is an advantage because your U.S. clients are curious and can't help but ask you some questions. The key is to allow the relationship to grow gradually. If you present yourself like the answer to all of their problems — before you even know their problems — then you are going to lack credibility with them.

When I was selling speakers, my goal was always to build the relationship first and to pitch my speaker second. The best case scenario is that you have a friendship happening before they even look at your materials. You want them to give you an honest answer about whether or not you are a contender.

> *Know the needs of your client well before you start providing solutions.*

FOLLOW UP

When you are following up with a client, don't be a stalker. If you have left several voice messages and not received a call back, try a quick query e-mail such as this:

> John, I've left a couple of messages — don't want you to think I'm a pest. Have you had a chance to review that e-mail I sent?

That's it. Not two or three lines about how great you are, just a question that they can hit reply and say, "Sorry, Jane, I haven't had a chance — touch base with me next week."

When you are following up with a client, don't be a stalker.

Never Assume You Know What's Happening at the Client's End

I have made this mistake many times. I thought a deal was dead because they hadn't returned calls. It just turned out that something more pressing was on the agenda and they came back to me later.

When you befriend your clients, you can ask them questions about your style and marketing materials and get an honest answer. Of course, every planner has different tastes and ten people might give you ten different answers.

Many planners appreciate a don't-waste-my-time, just-get-to-the-point style, while others might like to build a relationship with people they hire first. It's up to you to gauge the person's style.

Again, read up on sales and behavioral styles so that you can use your skills to build long-term relationships.

Ways to Stay Top of Mind

You might try a combination of phone calls, e-mail, and postcards to keep yourself top of mind with prospective clients. If you know they are close to making a decision, you might try to connect every four or five days, but if you are not sure then every two weeks is enough. If a client is not in decision mode, then once a month is plenty to touch base.

If I know a client is making a decision soon, my contact might go something like this:

Day 1 — send information (probably by e-mail)

Day 5 — e-mail check–in: "Did you get materials?"

Day 12 — phone call, if no response, voice mail: "Just checking to see if you've reviewed materials."

Day 19 — quick e-mail: "How are things going — did you get a chance to look over the materials?"

No response.

Day 26 — phone call: "Don't want to bug you, but I know your deadline is approaching. Is my speaker (or am I) being considered (or did we make the short list)?"

No response.

Day 33 — postcard: "Thanks for considering my speaker. I'll assume you are set and will be in touch for next year."

This final postcard let's them know that you understand the industry, don't take their lack of response personally, and are going to leave them alone now.

Right or wrong, this approach has worked for me in the past — but I will say this: *new times call for new approaches*. Be creative, try different approaches, and see what works for you.

2.0 WORK IT LIKE A FARMER

If you think about your business like a farmer's field, it might keep you moving forward. Your initial contact with the client is the stage where you are planting the seeds. It truly is a numbers game so planting seeds constitently will be key.

Next, comes fertilization. I can see where some of you might think that you need to pile on the s**t here, but I mean rich fertilizer. Something meaningful that you can send to say "keep me top of mind" or "I have good information for you." That might look like a copy of an article or a link to a blog post.

Top 12 Marketing Strategies

Here are a list of a dozen top strategies to keep you in your clients' thoughts.

1. Sales Calls or E-mail Queries — The call-send-call method (outlined previously in this chapter).

2. The Article Placement Strategy — Place articles in your target industry's publications and blogs.

3. Direct Mail — Series of postcards and articles.

4. Social Media — Pull people into your fan base with daily Tweets and updates that establish you as the expert.

> *When you have done enough seeding and enough fertilizing, that's when the harvest will come.*

5. Shake the Trees — Work your inner circle and past clients to drum up new business. You should be talking to past clients once a year to stay in touch.

6. Outbound Broadcasts — Send out newsletters and eTips that help drive people to your website and often they will result in business.

7. Quiz or Audit — Adding this feature to your website could tee up conversations that result in business.

8. Media Darling — be quoted as an expert and be seen by the media as someone who can comment on your specialty.

9. Freebie Speeches — Speak to anyone who will listen to generate momentum.

10. Marketing Calendar — Develop a 12-month system to ensure that you are "touching" clients on a regular basis.

11. Blogging — This was invented to help drive people to your website. Ensure that you are blogging consistently.

12. Public Seminars — Run your own public events to generate cash flow and gain access to companies.

THE OUTCOME

At some point a decision will be made — you will get the engagement or you won't. Remember, don't take it personally. You simply were not a match this year.

When a meeting planner tells you that you are not a good fit for their meeting this year, politely ask whether or not you will be considered in the future and schedule a call for next year. Don't argue or try to change their mind.

When I was working at the speakers' bureau, agents would often tell me about speakers getting angry on the phone when they were told they were not a fit. They had no idea the kind of impression this behavior left on the bureau agent. That agent, and that bureau, would *never* book that speaker now. And meeting planners feel similarly.

If they did not like your video, then you are going to have some work ahead of you to get another shot. That's why it's so important that your video is good and reflects you well.

Here are a few tips on handling rejection from actor and speaker Mike Pniewski.

> There is no doubt in my mind that actors are the most rejected people on the planet. Statistics from the Screen Actors Guild bear that out by concluding that 98% of their 100,000+ members can't make a decent living. So as I began my career, I knew I would need to prepare myself with a strategy that allowed me to keep the inevitable rejections from being an obstacle for myself. If I was going to be in that two percent, my focus needed to be on my goals and not the everyday frustrations. My strategy has three parts.
>
> First, rejection in business is never personal and that is always my choice. I have defined for myself very clearly what is business and what is personal in my life and understand that my work is all "business," even if it is a business about people. Second, I empower myself by having command of my craft. I do whatever it takes to be at the top of my game at all times by being properly trained and prepped, knowing what my "customer" wants, and having the right "tools" to do the job. Third, and most

importantly, I keep my priorities in order so that no rejection in my work cripples me to the point of being ineffective. My self-worth and purpose are controlled by me at all times.

This came in handy several years ago when I traveled to Los Angeles from my home in Atlanta to audition for the popular TV series *The West Wing*. It was a terrific role that had been difficult to cast to that point. When I got the call from my agent, he said the casting director told him I was perfect for it and would love me to come and meet with them. After reading the material, I was thrilled for the chance to audition for this part on such an acclaimed show. I was fully prepared when I went into their office and performed about as well as I could. The feedback in the moment from those in the room was very positive and they thanked me many times for coming. A couple of hours later my agent called and said they had picked someone else. They loved my work, thought I was great but I wasn't the one. Was I disappointed? Yes, this was not an inexpensive trip for an audition! But this is the nature of my work — sometimes you win and sometimes you don't. However, you'll never win if you don't take the shot.

After I processed this, I came out on the other end enormously grateful for the opportunity (hundreds of other actors would have given anything to be in my shoes!) and confident that the good impression I left will serve me well at some point in the future. Hopefully soon!

Mike has gone on to work in other great TV show, like *The Good Wife* and *Drop Dead Diva*, so he really walks his talk.

Building a Database

Everything you do in this business needs to have a strategy behind it. Here is a great question to post on your bulletin board: "Is this task getting me to where I want to go?" Many people spend time on the low pay-off activities and forget to do some of the most integral things that can help grow their business — like building a database.

From day one of your business, you should be adding names to a database and putting them into categories. Are they "speaking prospects," "book prospects," "friends," etc. You may want to categorize your clients by year (20XX Keynote Client) so it's easy to pull them all up at the end of the year to recap or to send holiday greetings. If you aren't putting names and addresses into a database, you are going to miss opportunities down the road.

My favorite contact management software, and the two that many speakers use are ACT! and Salesforce. You'll read more on this in Chapter 7 in the High-Tech Speaker on the Road section. It allows you to customize many fields for information that you are going to need each time you talk to a prospect, as well as information that you will merge later into a contract once the deal is closed. Here is some of the information for which you will want to set up fields.

- Organization (this and all of the standard info like address, etc., is already set up)
- Contact Name (if there are multiple meeting planners, you can easily set up a group)
- Date of Next Meeting (make sure that you put it in a format that you can easily search)
- Location of Next Meeting (what city)
- Planning Month (when will they be doing their planning)
- Number of Speakers (they use at their event)
- Fee Quoted
- Industry Type (you may want to set this up as a drop down list, again for easy searching)

Eventually, this information will lead to a contract and you'll have most of the information already in set fields so that you just merge the information into an agreement template.

On the other hand, if you intend to build your business online, you may also want to consider building your database in a shopping cart software. The one I use is called One Shopping Cart and it manages my credit card sales at the same time.

Before buying anything, think through your needs and your long-term goals. Knowing these factors will help you choose the software that is most effective for you. Whatever software you choose, make sure that the contacts can be downloaded into other applications, should you change your mind later on.

If you aren't putting names and addresses into a database, you are going to miss opportunities down the road.

2.0 DATABASE AND CONTACT MANAGEMENT

By the time the ink dries on this version of the book, this information will be outdated, so here's the latest *as of today*. There are several things to consider when building your database, and you'll most likely end up having lists in different places. Ideally, we house our information out "on the cloud" so that there's no longer a need to load bulky software onto our computers (see Technology Tips 2.0 by Masters Joe Heaps and Dave Reed, later in this chapter). When things are available "on the cloud" they allow more than one person to work within the program on your behalf.

Here's what you need.

- CRM/database System: This is what I've used ACT! for in the past. It gives you the option to keep every conversation with the client documented, brings sales call reminders and to do items into your calendar, merges documents with templates, etc. The best systems are customizable.

- Autoresponders: This is a way for you to group people so that you can send out broadcasts. Many speakers use Constant Contact or Mail Chimp, but I use my One Shopping Cart for this.

Ideally, we house our information out "on the cloud."

- Shopping Cart: If you want to sell product and accept credit cards you'll need this platform. Many shopping carts offer autoresponders.

- Name Squeeze: Where do the people who sign up for your newsletter go? For me, they get dropped right into a "Prospects" autoresponder within my One Shopping Cart.

You'll probably have a totally separate database of people in Social Media, but we'll keep that separate for now.

The only software that I know of so far that combines all of these together is called Infusionsoft. When I researched it last, it was a fairly expensive undertaking for a speaker who is just getting started, but perhaps reasonable if you had some traction ($300/month). You may opt for separate systems to get you started and move over to an integrated system later on.

WEBSITE REFERENCE TOOL

www.speakerlauncher.com ➡
Book Buyer LOGIN *(red button)*
Check Out: Salesforce, ACT!, Infusionsoft, One Shopping Cart

DATABASE BUILDING STRATEGIES

There are many ways to go about getting more people into your database. It's important to be clear about the purpose of your database. Are these people going to book you for speeches, are they going to buy products from you later on? If you intend to write a book that everyone in business would benefit from, then you'll want everyone from your business audiences to be added to your list.

You have a way to manage the contacts, now you need to add to your list. Take advantage of every speech using the following techniques.

- The "Help Me" Speech
- Feedback Forms
- Business Card Draw
- Help from the Meeting Planner
- All Roads Lead to Your Website — handouts, PowerPoint, dangle your carrot (newsletter)
- Social Media

The "Help Me" Speech: Ask for the Business

Thom Winninger, who is a master at getting spin-off gigs from each engagement, taught me something *huge* many, many years ago. I call it the "help me" speech and have tweaked it some, but many speakers have used Thom's technique effectively to build their businesses.

When you are nearing the end of your presentation, preferably right before your closing story, insert the "help me" statement, or something like it, to let the audience know that you do this for a living and you'd love their help. Here's the "help me" line:

> As you can see I am passionate about _____ (your topic). If you know of any company or association who could benefit from this material, please come and hand me your business card afterwards.

That's it. Two lines that if missed could cost you thousands in spin-off business from every single event. People want to help you and they also want a reason to come up and talk to you afterwards. So you are just allowing them to do what is natural and you are being specific about what they can do for you. When people hand you their cards, write down the details of what they say on the back (April event, 500 CEOs) so that you don't forget when you are following up. And one more thing … *Follow up!*

> *A Note about the "Help Me" Speech:* There are speakers who feel strongly that the "help me" speech is not a great idea for some corporate audiences. The meeting planner hired you to do a job and although it's only two lines, it's inappropriate. I would suggest that you be more vigilant about doing the help me speech in the beginning of your career and, most especially, when you are doing free speeches. Later in your career, it may no longer be necessary or appropriate. Bottom line, you are asking for the business and you'll have to decide whether or not to do it and how to go about it. Be creative.

My first job in the industry was with Betska K-Burr, a leadership expert. Betska was a really smart business woman who had come out of 3M. She taught me a lot about business. The one thing that helped us grow so quickly was that she was great at asking for business from the platform. When I started working for her, she handed me a huge stack of business cards. They were all warm leads that she had collected giving her "help me" speech. I spent my first three months working with Betska following up those warm leads and they filled our pipeline for the next three years.

I have an extremely high-tech gathering device for collecting those business cards — the one and only plastic Ziploc baggie, usually snack size. I put a label on it — name of event and date — before going to the event and come back with a baggie full of leads. After I have followed up and added them to my database, they go back into the baggie, in case I ever need to track a business card down.

Feedback Forms

Getting the entire audience list could be beneficial. Using a feedback form guarantees most of the audience will respond and you'll get information beyond a database entry. There are five uses for feedback forms:

1. to find out what the audience likes and doesn't like about your presentation,

2. to gather testimonials,

3. to gather names and contact information for your database,

4. to get referrals, and

5. to get more business with this audience.

Every speaker bombs every once in awhile. Know that you are not alone.

• • • • • • • • • • •

1. **Audience Feedback** — Asking your audience what they liked and what can be improved about your speech is very helpful, especially in the beginning of your career. Resist the urge to concentrate on the 1% of negative feedback when you have 99% positive. But always ask yourself if the information could be useful to you. You will rarely please 100% of the people in your audience, so don't be too concerned about every piece of negative feedback. Always be willing to learn and grow. Every speaker bombs every once in awhile. Know that you are not alone.

2. **Testimonials** — When asking for testimonials, ask the question, "What will you do differently as a result of this presentation?" or "What have you learned that you will apply?" We want testimonials rich with ROI not a bunch saying "You are a good speaker." Every speaker has those.

3. **Database Building** — When asking for contact information, be sure to gather the minimum data — name and e-mail and, if possible, mailing address. Having addresses on file will allow you some flexibility in your marketing down the road.

4. **Referrals** — Although you do your "help me" speech, you can also ask for referrals on your feedback form. The standard line, "Who do you know who could benefit from this material?" would work.

5. **More Business with this Audience** — You could ask the group what else you might do for them and list the topics that you could come back to deliver at a later date.

Try your feedback form a few times and then tweak it. If you find you're not getting enough back, you might be asking for too much.

Be strategic about every event. Ask, "How can I turn this into more business?"

A short keynote may not be as appropriate for a feedback form, but you do want to leave some sort of paper trail whenever possible that includes your contact information and URL. Be strategic about every event. Ask, "How can I turn this into more business?"

Business Card Draw

An easy way to collect contact information from every person in the audience is to arrange a business card draw with the meeting planner. After your speech the planner can bring up the basket and have you make the draw. Then, you take home all of the cards and all of those people become prospects for your next product. You should announce from the platform that if they do not wish to be added to your database to make a note on their card. If you are giving away some of your back of room materials, try to do the draw before the first break, otherwise people will wait to purchase from you until the end of the session.

Help from the Meeting Planner

The meeting planner is your partner on the event, so you'll want to collaborate with him or her and offer up all of the things that you can do to add value to the event. In order to keep your message alive, you might ask the meeting planner to send out a follow up e-mail after your speech. You can include a few more tips in the e-mail (value), as well as your URL (you want to drive people to your website). The meeting planner may also provide you with the list of names to do the e-mail yourself. Be respectful of these situations and make sure that you don't start spamming groups of people. Trust me when I say that unauthorized use of any list will come back to haunt you. Anytime I have been overzealous in my marketing in the past, it has backfired. Always get permission to send an e-mail to a past audience. Once they hand over their business card, there may be an unspoken agreement that they'll be added to your list, but you'd be wise to mention it and allow them to opt out.

You might also ask the meeting planner if he or she is interested in publishing any of your articles before or after your presentation. This is great added value for the organization and keeps your name alive with the group for as long as possible.

All Roads Lead to Your Website

Any speaking engagement is an opportunity to drive potential clients to your website. Your website should have some way of collecting names and e-mail addresses (see dangling carrot below) of the visitors who come to your site. There are entire online strategies available from some of the Internet gurus. Do your homework and learn all of the methods, then decide what is best for you. When you are collecting information online, you might ask only for name, e-mail, and state or province. It's helpful to know where they live in case you run seminars there. Below are some methods to encourage attendees to visit your site.

- **Paper Trail** — Leaving a paper trail is a great way to ensure that you'll get some activity on your website after each speech. Leaving behind anything from a handout to a workbook, bookmark, promotional product (pen, calendar, postcard, etc.) or even a sports card is a good idea. Try to keep your give-away at a low per-unit cost, since your audience numbers will climb.

- **PowerPoint** — Your presentation should advertise your website without going too far. It should be present, but not overwhelming. Just remember to keep it balanced.

- **Dangling Your Carrot/Newsletter** — While on the platform, you want to entice your audience to head on over to your website to get your freebie (see Phase II: Aim, under Your Website). That will get them directly into your database. Between your business card draw, PowerPoint, handouts, and carrot, people from your audiences should be able to find you.

- **Social Media** — Many speakers will ask their audience to follow them on Twitter or Facebook. You might even use

Twitter during your presentations to engage the audience. The goal? Pull people into your fan base and keep them there until they buy from you. Technology expert Scott Klososky uses a technology called Join Speaker from the platform to have the audience ask questions live. How cool is that? (See Scott's Flashpoint in Chapter 7.)

> *Bottom Line*: When you are paid to speak at an event, you must first provide value, then people will be more inclined to help you get spin-off. Being too pushy or aggressive diminishes the value that you have provided.

What If I Work Alone?

If you are a sole proprietor reading this, you're probably thinking, "Yeah right, I have time to follow up with every client this way." That's okay. If you are working this business on your own and have no desire to hire and manage staff, then you are going to want a different approach. Your operation will need to be an easy, flowing system with many of your processes prepared ahead of time.

SYSTEMS IN PLACE

You'll need to plan ahead so that you can manage the business while taking care of business. Below are some ideas that will help get you set and keep you moving along.

- Your speech must be great, so that you don't need to market as much.
- You need to have processes in place to follow up leads and not let potential business fall through the cracks.
- Your "help me" speech must be a part of every presentation. (See the Database Building Strategies earlier in this chapter.)
- Have templates built into your e-mail system for everything. That way, when a client gets in touch, you have something ready. If you want to send the client information that is specific to his or her organization such as testimonials, then you

might send those separately to stay top of mind and to keep your process as quick and easy as possible.

- Have a virtual bookkeeper or someone in your neighborhood set up to do invoicing and travel expenses for you. Put a 4 × 6 brown envelope into every client file with the essential information printed on the outside — client name, address, date of event. Fill in the airfare, ground travel, hotel and miscellaneous expenses, placing the receipts into the envelope and putting it into the bookkeeper's "In" basket. You can set up a template in ACT! that will merge the client's name, event date, etc., right onto this form.

- When you return from a trip your file should contain a Ziploc baggie full of business card leads from your "help me" speech and the brown expenses envelope. The business card leads need to be entered into your database (another $10-$12/hour job for someone that can be done locally or virtually). You might even do this yourself on the plane ride home.

- Send thank you cards to the meeting planner and bureau. You might have two or three postcards placed in each file with labels printed from the ACT! file before you go. If you want to go electronic with this, sendoutcards.com will do the sending for you!

- *This is most important.* Follow up with those people who gave you their business cards! Drop them a line over e-mail on the plane. These are hot leads. Every day that goes by diminishes the heat. Follow up within two to three days.

CONSISTENCY IS KEY

You may be losing business simply because you are not doing things in a consistent manner.

All of the ideas in this book are useful, but only if you follow through on them with some consistency. Discipline is hard for many of us, but I've learned that without it, your office can fall apart very quickly. You may be losing business simply because you are not doing things in a consistent manner. When things start slipping through the cracks, eventually it leads to client's not being serviced properly, deals lost or something worse that makes you miss an engagement.

You're Booked — Now What?

You've got a booking. That's great! Give yourself a pat on the back — now back to work. Not only do you need to prepare for the engagement so all is in place, you will still have work to do after you've received your standing O.

FLOW OF THE BOOKING

Every time you book an engagement, a series of things should fall into place — either by doing them yourself or with help. As mentioned earlier, consistency is key so develop a system with a checklist and stick to it.

- **Agreement and Invoice** — (See Chapter 7 for Agreements and Contracts.) Agreements are a top priority because they bring in money and confirm that the client is serious. Agreements will always be the first and most important document you create. You may want to send a copy of your book (or other product) with every agreement to plant the seed about quantity discounts, so that they pre-purchase books for everyone. Leave a copy of the agreement in the file so that you can ensure that you follow through on what you have promised the client. If you have promised books or something extra as a part of the deal, then make a calendar note to ship them two weeks prior to the event and put a reminder in the file. Never rely on your memory because eventually all of your engagements will run together, so you must have procedures in place to ensure that nothing falls through the cracks.

- **Client Folder** — If you aren't 100% electronic yet, prepare and label a client file folder. Keep your client files a different color so that they are easy to spot among other files. You might use a color that signifies wealth to you, like green or purple. Your label should have the client name, the date and the city, so that five years from now — after several repeat engagements — you know which gig is which. You may want to do this electronically — just be sure you have reminders that "pop up." Print some extra labels.

- **Leads Baggie/Envelope** — While you are making your label for the file, make a second one for the leads baggie or envelope.

- **Thank You Cards** — And since you are making labels, you might as well make address labels for the client and the bureau and put them on your thank you card envelopes. It's perfectly acceptable to hand write these from the road if you prefer. Don't forget to add the postage so you can hand them over to the hotel staff or drop them in a mailbox from the road.

- **Contact Management** — Make sure that you tag your client properly in ACT! (or whatever contact management software you use), so that you can easily reference all clients for that year at once.

- **Event Details Form** — You may develop this document using merge files from an ACT! database or you may wait until right before you travel and download the info from eSpeakers. (More on eSpeakers in Chapter 7.) An Event Detail Form includes all of the information from the agreement: client details, event details, travel details, flights, ground, hotel and any other pertinent information.

- **Expenses Envelope** — Again, because this is all personalized with the name of the client and the date you should do this all at once.

- **Handouts** — If you know at this point what handout you will use, then place the original in the file. You may want to send the original with your contract, along with your bio, introduction, photo and pre-program questionnaire if you have one. All of these items may be available on the meeting planners page on your website. Keep a spare copy of your introduction in the file. The MC will often forget to bring a copy to the meeting.

- **Product Ship Date** — Schedule a product ship date and make notes on what you plan to send.

That's a summary of what needs to go into your client file before you hit the road. We're getting everything set up as a system. Refer to your checklist at least six hours before departure. No leaving it to the last minute in case there is something pertinent missing! Having a checklist that you refer to before departure will ensure you are not showing up frazzled for your speech.

Having a checklist that you refer to before departure will ensure you are not showing up frazzled for your speech.

MAKING THE MOST OF EACH SPEAKING ENGAGEMENT

Your work is not complete just because you received a standing O. You need to be thinking ahead — to the next booking, or your overall contact with this client. Is there more work here to be done? Perhaps some consulting? Here are some ideas that can help increase your chances of more business spinning off from each presentation. These should also be a part of your process so that you are never missing opportunities.

- Once the client has chosen you for the presentation, ask them how long they want your message to resonate with their audience? They should say "as long as possible" and this tees you up to talk about how you might develop some depth and continuity to your speech by placing articles in their publications before and after your speech or doing more training.

- Offer to meet with an inside group of people before your speech for a meal or a special workshop (this might include the Executive Group, Board of Directors, Inner Circle, etc.).

- Request a meeting with the Big Cheese (President, CEO, Executive Director) and find out during that meeting how you can customize your presentation to help them in their mission. This also adds to your credibility once on stage because you sound like you are buddies with the boss.

- Immediately following your presentation, ask the meeting planner to send a follow-up e-mail from you to the group.

You can add a few points that you missed or didn't have time for and direct them to other articles of interest on your website. You can also point them to your online store. If the meeting planner is open to giving you the e-mail addresses, then you may send the e-mail directly to them.

- As we said earlier, having a door prize draw during your presentation allows you to collect the business cards of everyone in the audience for a giveaway. This will showcase your product — hopefully your book, or whatever prize you give away — and give you all of the audience's business cards. The biggest issue will be getting these people added to your database in a timely fashion.

- Use your "Help Me" speech. (See Building a Database earlier in this chapter.)

- When you are talking to the client about your speech, find out what other meetings take place throughout the year and the purpose of each — you might fit into those as well. Also talk about initiatives that the company is undertaking and plant seeds about what you can help them with.

- Thank them for their business after your speech. You might send a gift along with your thank you note at this time or you might wait and send a gift during a holiday. A copy of your book may or may not qualify as a gift. Hopefully by the end of your engagement you know something about them so that you can personalize it.

- Make your follow-up call to the client a week or two after your presentation.
  - Ask them what has changed as a result of your presentation. If they start listing things, ask if you can quote them and send them an e-mail confirming what they said. This prevents you waiting for a testimonial letter.
  - Ask them how you can support them in the future.
  - Ask who else they know who could benefit from your material — other departments in their company or other chapters of their association, colleagues, etc.

– Schedule a follow-up call or a note in the future. A quick e-mail asking how things are going six months later may put you in line for more business.

THE MINNESOTA FATS APPROACH

I heard about the Minnesota Fats Approach at NSA. The idea is that, like the legendary pool player Minnesota Fats, you are not only focusing on the shot that you are making, but on the next two or three follow up shots. You're planning ahead.

When I worked at International Speakers' Bureau in Dallas as an agent, I wanted to work with speakers who would help me close business and cue me up for future business. I was speaking with a client who was in need of some sales training and I immediately thought of a speaker named Jim Pancero. I sent the client to his website, while we were talking on the phone, and she said he looked like he might be a good fit. She had also mentioned that they had a new product launch in three months and I knew that new products were one of Jim's specialties. She was excited. I had Jim call the client the next day. He closed that deal for me and the deal for the new product launch. No videos were exchanged and the contract was in place within 48 hours of the initial contact. It was a bureau agent's dream deal. Jim and I teamed up for the Minnesota Fat's Approach — cue up the second ball, while pocketing the first.

2.0 EXPANDING BEYOND THE SPEECH

In today's market, we must always be thinking beyond the speech. Yes, that may get our foot in the door, but how can we move into a long-term relationship with this client to get the maximum results from our content? Some new ideas for expanding your brand beyond the speech might include:

- An add-on follow-up package that involves customized video messages to the participants turning your one-day event into a six- or twelve-month training program.
- Monthly calls with the audience so they can join your club or membership program to get more time with you.

- An additional session with a special group, such as a leadership retreat following your session.

- Put a program into place where they bring your message all the way into the organization with promotional products (posters, coffee mugs, door knockers).

- Additional training to further hit home the message. If people are really serious about change, then one session may not be enough.

- If they need more time with you, have a brainstorming style session on your menu that allows them to pick your brain for the day. The more time you spend with them, the more likely they will incorporate your message fully.

2.0 KNOW YOUR REVENUE FLOW

Ideally, we want to be clear about how our revenue can start with a client and what it might lead to. It can happen in various scenarios, but it might start with an association keynote, then several companies hire you for consulting, which leads to some training and product sales. Check out my example of the umbrella (see Figure A in Chapter 1 under So What Else Is New?) with the revenue flow and think about what's perfect for you. Use the blank version below (Figure I) to create your own scenarios.

 COACH'S QUESTION: *How many opportunities (for speeches, consulting, training or coaching) did I let slip through my fingers because I was focused on closing one speech?*

Did you follow up on all the leads you received after your gig or have they cooled off? Did you spend enough time investigating the training opportunities with that fellow from AT&T? Have you followed up on that successful gig with the Missouri Bankers and asked for a referral for their national conference?

FIGURE I: **Your Revenue Flow**

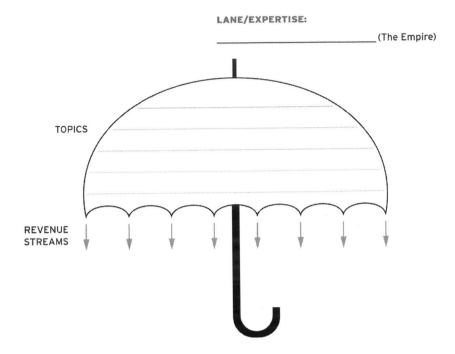

6

SPEAKERS' BUREAUS AND EVENT PLANNING COMPANIES

Event Planning Companies

Now that you have been booking your gigs on your own for a few years, you might want to enlist the help of our industry's intermediaries. These are the companies that help corporate and association meeting planners put together their events.

There are many different types of agencies. A client may use a *destination management* (DM) company to help with the location. Or they may hire an *event planner* to deal with everything from speakers to table settings. A *production company* may step in to do the staging and all of the audio visual components and they may even provide the talent. These companies may have an in-house speakers' bureau or they may work with speakers' bureaus.

When working with event companies, either directly or through bureaus, here are a few things to keep in mind.

1. It would be a bad idea to discuss your fee with the end-user client. The production company or DM has put together a package deal for the group that includes speakers and they may or may not have marked up your fee.

2. Understand that you are a very small part of a much larger production. Do your best to be easy-going.

3. Be organized and give them everything they need from you in a timely manner (e.g., AV needs, introductions, photos, outlines, etc.).

4. Understand that production companies have some great clients and building the relationship with the people behind the camera and lighting is as important as the executives.

5. Make sure you understand what happens to spin-off from these events. If the client calls you directly for more business, the originating company should hear about it and have the option to draw up the contract. The same goes for product sales. Some may ask for a percentage. You're best to treat them similarly to a bureau.

Production company executive, André Shahrdar, Director of Sales at Barkley Kalpak Associates, Inc., had this to say about working with speakers:

> The most important thing that a speaker should know when working with a client like us is that for the period of time we are engaging this person to speak, they represent us entirely. They represent our professionalism, our brand, our staff and, ultimately, they hold our relationship with our client in their hands. Therefore, it is paramount that the speaker understands our ultimate goal is to support the client's objective in conveying a specific message at a meeting or an event. We have to feel extremely confident that the speaker thoroughly grasps that message, the organization and the audience. He or she must be keenly focused on the goal of supporting that message. We look for expertise, the ability to engage an audience and flexibility in approach. Our most successful speakers have been those who listened carefully during their first meeting with us and then provided a customized approach at the first client meeting.

Kris Young, at Martin Bastian Productions, has this to say about the incredible waste of time and money that results from events that lack purpose and focus.

Tips from the Masters: *KRIS YOUNG*

Helping Clients Turn Good Events into Memorable Ones

I believe in the potential power of corporate meetings and events. However, as stated in our book *Never By Chance* (Wiley, 2010), I continue to think that meetings and events are, for most companies, a hidden asset that they rarely take full advantage of. The fact is there is no form of communication that will engage people with a shared vision more effectively than simply bringing their people together.

The challenge is that successful and effective meetings don't happen just because the speaker was great, the venue was perfect, or the food was good. The bulk of the work behind a focused and purposefully designed meeting or event actually happens up front through serious conversation around the "why" and the "how" of the event (conversations that should include the speakers, as well).

In a perfect world, organizations would always know exactly what they want to accomplish and how they plan to advance their strategy with the opportunity of their next event. I say Production Companies, Planners, Speakers, Speakers Bureaus, and Agencies take a stand. It's time we help our clients to invest time in planning and designing events that will make a significant difference in their business or organization.

Avoiding the following mistakes will help you and your client's further this cause.

Note the added "tips" meant especially for speakers.

TEN MEETING MISTAKES AND WAYS WE CAN HELP CLIENT'S AVOID THEM

1. Having a meeting just because you always have a meeting.

   Tip: This helps no one and rarely results in any kind of success. Sounds wrong, but consider the obvious (you may be thanked later). Gently suggest: "Save your money until the reason for having the meeting is clear."

2. Going into the meeting without stated objectives and a clearly defined outcome.

    Tip: Continue to ask "What's the point?"

3. Not utilizing a production company that understands how to help design and produce an effective, strategic event and make the most of your investment.

    Tip: Have the name of a really good meeting design company handy to suggest to a client who is ready to take things up a notch.

4. Putting more focus on what the executives or speakers want to say than what the audience needs to hear.

    Tip: As speakers you go to more meetings than anyone. Pay attention to the structure and design of the entire event. Offer advice where you can. Consider how you are integrated into the overall event. Is there a more effective way? What might the audience need to hear from you?

5. Overloading the schedule without giving participants time to network, process, and just catch their breath.

    Tip: Here is a great place for speakers to offer up good advice. You often know best when the audience may need to process what they just heard or share ideas that may have percolated during your presentation. Suggest an idea-swap break, a Q&A, or time to process.

6. Focusing on only one mode of communicating (i.e., a podium parade of talking heads) as opposed to looking at multiple ways to communicate and engage the audience.

    Tip: Good content often goes to waste when the audience is not engaged. Never stop challenging yourself on this. There are so many ways to engage an audience these days. Here's one: a shorter presentation. Think about it. Is every moment of your presentation necessary?

7. Poor coordination and communication between/among speakers, resulting in conflicting messages or unnecessary repetition.

   Tip: Speakers should be asking their clients about who else might be on the program. Little things (like referring back to another speaker's point or building on a previous story) can make a big impact. Ask to talk to other speakers before the event.

8. Making no provision for building on the meeting's objectives and goals after the event.

   Tip: There is huge opportunity here.

9. Structuring the event so that the audience is completely passive, not allowing them to interact and affect the meeting and its content.

   Tip: Much is lost when people have to wait until they get home to share an idea. Being able to share an idea with a co-worker, executive, or even a speaker in the moment can be a catalyst to change the energy in the room or even result in a breakthrough.

10. Not updating the meeting's structure to reflect changes in the company, the audience, or the culture at large.

   Tip: A great way to engage your audience is to surprise them. If they walk into the same old meeting environment it can defeat the purpose of taking them out of their everyday work environment. An element of surprise or disruption can be a great way to open up to new ideas.

Master Kris Young *is the Director of Speakers & Entertainment at Martin Bastian Productions. She helps create experiences for audiences.*

2.0 MEETING PLANNING COMPANIES

These companies have not been immune to hardship over the past few years and many are not doing nearly the level of business that they did in "the good old days." Companies are bringing the planning in-house to save money, or they are cancelling their events all together.

Working with Speakers' Bureaus

Many speakers are scratching their heads and wondering how to break into the elusive speakers' bureau network. Either the bureaus never call you or they call and place holds and you never get booked. By the end of this chapter you should be very clear on when you are ready to work with bureaus, what to expect when you do start, and how to build long-term relationships.

2.0 SPEAKERS' BUREAUS

Like the event companies, the bureaus are fighting the economy *and* technology. Web-based searching makes it easier than ever to find resources and speakers. The success of a speakers' bureau in the 2.0 climate will come down to their relationships with clients and their ability to innovate. Those that are flourishing are doing so because they are willing to change, update, and expand beyond speeches.

> *Like the event companies, the bureaus are fighting the economy and technology.*

BUILDING YOUR BUSINESS ON YOUR OWN

The best approach to getting bureaus to notice you is to go about building your business on your own. Vince and I discovered this when I started working with him.

Vince Poscente and I had to be very careful when working with bureaus in the early days because they didn't trust us. Mostly because Vince's wife Michelle owned a bureau. Word got out that Vince was a great speaker and we started to build a solid non-bureau (direct) business. Slowly the bureaus started to take notice and the business grew. He started getting booked into bigger audiences and with better clients.

One bureau that I really wanted to work with was National Speakers Bureau in Chicago. Brian Palmer, the owner, was a tough nut to crack. He was extremely selective about the speakers he would book. After three or four years of us working the business ourselves, National Speakers Bureau noticed that they were losing business to us and they called. We began a relationship that grew over time and they became one of our best clients. Had we tried to force that relationship in the beginning, we would have turned them off and they would have never started to work with us. If you are good, bureaus will start to lose business to you and that will get their attention.

The best approach to getting bureaus to notice you is to go about building your business on your own.

2.0 ⚡ FLASHPOINT: Gail Davis, GDA Speakers Bureau

Before I founded GDA Speakers, I was the director of corporate incentives at Electronic Data Systems, also known as EDS, or even more famously, Ross Perot's company. Today, it's now part of HP. EDS made Perot a billionaire. We had high standards, worked hard, and the sales teams were closing huge multi-year contracts worth millions. It meant big budgets for our events and a willingness to pay for a speaker, no questions asked.

...That was 15 years ago. Today the need for speakers has remained steady, but the clients' expectations for flexibility and generosity are higher. For example, they ask for the speaker to lower their fees or throw in books. While we believe in fee integrity, we also believe in keeping our clients. That's why we're all in business! Our approach to counter this trend has been to offer more for the same rate. For example, ask the speaker to attend a reception or do a seminar for a small group of top leadership either in person or via conference or video call after the event as a follow-up. Or is it possible to plan the meeting date to coincide with a time when the speaker is already in the area? This saves on travel. Bringing flexible, creative thinking to the deal is how you turn leads into clients.

RULES OF ENGAGEMENT

This is your business and it's your decision who to market to and who to work with. If you don't want to work with bureaus and don't want to give away 25% in commission, then don't. If you don't want to pay a 30% commission — then don't. Get clear on your rules of engagement and be consistent about applying them.

*If you are good, bureaus will start to lose business to you and **that** will get their attention.*

Many speakers will complain about bureaus and then when the bureau calls with a booking, all of their complaints mysteriously vanish.

You will find that almost every relationship succeeds or fails based on how close your values match up to your partners'. Bureaus are no exception. Work with bureaus who believe in doing business the same way that you do. If you are all about honesty and integrity then find bureaus — or bureau agents — who value those qualities as well. In the early stages of your career, you'll probably take business that you'll regret and you'll work with people that you don't like, but sort through the relationships and reject the ones that aren't working for you. Hopefully you are not biting the hand that has fed you for years and helped you build your business in the first place. It's very difficult to turn your back on the people who were integral in building your business, so if you do end the relationship make sure you do it tactfully and honestly.

A DAY IN THE LIFE OF A BUREAU AGENT

This is based on my own experience working under the roof of a speakers' bureau for six years. Obviously this is a skewed version, but hopefully it will help you understand bureaus and the demands on agents a little better.

Arrive in the office after a 30-minute commute and grab my second coffee. Minimal water cooler talk — work to do. Boot up computer. Seventy-five new e-mail messages — scour to find that there are three from clients. Listen to voice mail — two clients leave message about gigs I'm working on — three speakers want to chat.

Make phone calls all morning — check first on clients who are in decision mode. Out of 20 clients — connect with three and leave voice mail for others. Return e-mail messages from the three clients and place other 72 e-mails in "review later" file. Must put together proposals for two clients — start researching ideas.

Mail comes in. Receive several packages from speakers — place them in the bin in Sara's office with the other 20 packages. We're about three months behind on reviewing speaker videos. (See 2.0 update on this below.)

Lunch Time — today all the agents bring lunches and gather in boardroom for new speaker review. Ten new speakers to review. Watch two to three minutes of first three videos and they generate little interest — nothing new. Really like two of the ten speakers and will ask Sara to get more information about them. One of them might be a fit for a client of mine, but I need to do more homework before I'll feel comfortable booking them.

Find bureaus that have similar values to yours and you will create enjoyable, long-term relationships.

There's a stir in the office, a bell rings. One of the other agents has booked a speaker. I've only rung the bell three times this month. So after a quick congratulations, I get back to work.

Afternoon — get my proposals ready to go out via e-mail with links to video; and one is an e-mail proposal. Clients that use to book solely on my recommendations are now asking to see speakers live or to watch video. Clients are nervous and need to justify how corporate dollars are being spent. I may spend several months working with this client, going back and forth with ideas. Sometimes they go with another bureau and sometimes they go in-house. I might spend three months working the deal and only make $500 once my boss takes the bureau's cut of the commission.

Late Afternoon — back on the phone returning calls to clients and speakers with whom I am trying to book business. Messages from speakers who I don't know go into the "return later" pile.

Leave office at 6:30. Commute is worse in afternoon traffic — home by 7:30.

In my early days at the bureau, we were all in our early 30s and none of us were married. We all worked until at least 7 p.m. each night. Building a business of any kind takes a lot of work and dedication. I know bureau owners who work alone. They put in ridiculous hours just to keep up with the mail!

I've provided this information scenario for you for two reasons: so you'll understand why they might not return your call and how hard they work to close one piece of business.

2.0 A DAY IN THE LIFE OF A BUREAU AGENT

Where before a bureau agent might get 75 e-mails, that could easily be doubled now. With every speaker (and his dog) having a newsletter, a large percentage of the e-mails are something that they didn't sign up for. (Be sure to ask permission before adding someone to your newsletter broadcast list.) Less and less these days will a bureau agent be FedExing a package with videos in it. Most proposals would go out via e-mail with links to video.

Where before a bureau was competing against other bureaus, now they are competing with other bureaus *and* every speaker out there, even the ones that have only been in business for half an hour. That should be reason enough alone for companies and associations to use bureaus — who wants to sort through all of the people out there on the Internet! Not me. Yikes!

WHY GIVE A PERCENTAGE AWAY?

Typically you will pay a speakers' bureau a commission of 25% to 30%. In my early days of representing speakers, I discovered that it took an average of 40 to 50 calls per day, five days per week to make our goal of 80 bookings per year. The calls-per-day number will go up or down depending on the speaker's level of talent and the marketing materials. I decided it would make more sense to educate 50 bureau people on how to sell my speaker than for me to make the calls. I wanted to leverage my time. I set out to work the bureau market with Vince and within three years, we built our business to almost 80% bureau bookings. Financially, that made sense for us, but if I were doing it again, I'd probably aim for 40%. You'll need to decide what percentage is right for you.

ARE YOU READY?

Unless you're a celebrity, most speakers' bureaus are not going to launch your career. They will most likely start paying attention to you after you have built a name for yourself.

To see if you are ready to work with bureaus, ask yourself the following questions:

- Have I given 30 or more paid speeches per year for at least two years? Or do I have some level of expertise or celebrity that overides this?

- Is my fee high enough? $3,500 is an average minimum, but some bureaus require $5,000.

- Are my materials ready (demo video, website, etc.) and do they sell me?

- Am I really good? Am I getting two or three spin-off engage-ments from each speech?

If you are wondering why your fee has to be at a certain level, all you need to do is crunch the numbers. Bureaus charge a commission of 25% to 30%. I do know a few bureaus who are higher, but these are average. The bureau owner may also split that commission with the agent in the office who books you. So let's take a $1000 fee, for exam-ple. The commission might be $300 and the bureau owner and agent might split that. Well, no one is making any money here, considering that it might take 50 to 100 phone calls to book one contract. The agent needs to focus where the money is — higher priced speakers.

If you are wondering why your fee has to be at a certain level, all you need to do is crunch the numbers.

Where Do I Find the Bureaus?

The easiest way to start is with the International Association of Speakers' Bureaus (IASB). They have a website *www.isabweb.org* and you can use their bureau locator to see the entire list of bureaus. From there, you'll want to do some research to narrow the list to bureaus who meet your criteria. Some criteria might be: they work with speakers in my genre and fee range; they have a great reputation in the industry, both with speakers and clients; and they have the type of clients that I want to work with. There is no point getting listed with a bureau that does all college work when you have no desire to speak to colleges.

WEBSITE REFERENCE TOOL

www.speakerlauncher.com ➡
Book Buyer LOGIN *(red button)*
Check Out: International Association of Speakers' Bureaus (IASB).

Getting Your Foot in the Door

The best scenario is for the bureau to have heard your name three times (preferably from clients or from other speakers) prior to you calling them. Have your clients and speaker buddies call on your behalf. Clients hold much more water when it comes to referrals.

Getting Listed

Getting listed means very little really. You are placed in their database with the other thousands of speakers. This is just the very first step in building your bureau relationship. Most bureaus post their requirements for getting listed with them on their websites. Check out the website first, then call and make sure your topic and fees are in line with what they book. If they give you the thumbs up, then send your materials. Write "as requested" in the subject line of the e-mail. Check back with them to see when your materials will be reviewed and get their feedback.

Staying Top of Mind

As noted above, getting listed is the first step. Now you want to take the relationship further. You need to stay in touch, but not become a stalker or pest. Every bureau will have their own preferences on how to be contacted, so make notes in your database and try to accommodate their wishes.

Clients and bureaus are looking to book you because of your style, your experience, your content and how it will benefit their audience.
— Theresa Beenken, National Speakers Bureau, Toronto, Ontario

- **Phone** — Calling to touch base during an agent's sales hours is probably not ideal, unless you have something important to say. Leaving after hours voice messages could be effective, however. Never call the bureau on their 1-800 line. Why should they pay for you to sell them an idea?

- **E-Mail** — The average number of e-mails a bureau agent receives per day is staggering. So when sending e-mail, make sure it has value for them; keep it short with links to more information; and never send anything weekly unless asked.

- **Mail** — Postcards and notes via old-fashioned snail mail also work.

- **In Person** — Visiting a bureau's office or inviting them to see you speak can really help build the relationship. Social settings are even better.

You'll need to work hard to keep the bureaus' attention. The more creative you can be the better. Below are some ideas to get the bureau agent's attention.

Showcases

If the bureau has showcases (which usually cost you money), that is a good way to gain some exposure to the bureau. Ideally, you want that bureau's agents, as well as their clients, to see you in action. Ask several speakers how many engagements they booked as a result of previous showcases before you pay your money.

If you are an unknown speaker and a bureau approaches you to showcase with them, be *very* cautious. They may be

*If you are an
unknown speaker
and a bureau
approaches you to
showcase with
them, be very
cautious.*

making more money from the showcases than from actually booking speakers. If you wait until a bureau books you before participating in a showcase, then you will be taking the safest route.

IASB has their own showcase during their annual convention in April. If you are working with some bureaus who are members, they might be able to get you onto the showcase — in front of all of the bureau agents and owners. The best case scenario is to have a bureau champion you as a main stage speaker at that event.

Handing Over Business

Another way to get noticed by a bureau is to hand them a deal that you have already closed. This might work if you are already close to getting in with the bureau and just want to tip it over the edge. But if the bureau doesn't know you and hasn't expressed any interest in you to date, I'd hold off.

Spiffs and Contests

A "spiff" is a contest or promotion that you would offer to the bureau agents to get them to book you more often. It might come in the form of a gift, like an iPod, a trip, etc. I've even seen some speakers offer cash. The idea is that the bureau agent who books the speaker the most would win. Sometimes there could be more than one winner.

I know speakers who currently run spiffs very successfully and it is a legal business practice. You just have to look at other industries to see that spiffs happen all of the time: a radio station offers a trip to the advertisers who spend the most money; a paper manufacturer takes all of their clients to a baseball game. But like doctors being wooed by pharmaceutical companies, there are certainly some grey areas. Is the client still getting the right speaker for the job?

Some bureaus are adamantly opposed to spiffs and you would do more damage than good suggesting one. Contests will definitely not work if you are a new speaker to that bureau. You must have a relationship first.

I did a survey of 50 bureau agents to find out what they thought about spiffs since they seemed to be somewhat controversial. Of the respondents, 40% of the bureaus said they don't believe spiffs are in the best interest of their clients; 37% said they participate when the speaker is the right fit for the client; 23% said that they participate only when they know the speaker *and* when the speaker is a fit for their client. Most bureau agents will put their clients' needs well above any incentive you can dangle in front of them.

Brad Plumb, CMP from Five Star Speakers and Trainers, said the following: "In my mind spiffs only work when a relationship is already developed with the agent, but not to introduce yourself to the agent. I would be shooting myself in the foot if the fit wasn't right for the client. Spiffs make me think of the speaker more often and it's kind of fun to be involved with a contest. In a bureau the size of Five Star, it creates a 'buzz' among the agents."

BTW, Five Stars has now gone bankrupt, which just goes to show that the economy hits all areas.

My job is to help you sort out the industry hoopla, so my best advice on spiffs is *proceed with caution*. Don't try spiffs if you are not known to bureaus. Ask them how they feel about spiffs before offering one up. If you do run a spiff, try to make it something that allows you to spend time with the bureau agent. With larger bureaus, you might offer an incentive for them to compete among themselves. Always clear the offer with the owner of the bureau first.

> *Most bureau agents will put their clients' needs well above any incentive you can dangle in front of them.*

Paying to Be Reviewed

Several years ago, bureaus were looking for a way to weed out some of the speakers that were approaching them. They would get 500 to 1000 new packets of speaker information per year to review. It was simply overwhelming and created a huge administrative challenge. Some bureaus decided that a way to cut it back was to charge to have speakers' materials reviewed. Their theory was that only speakers who were serious would spend the money.

If a bureau charges to look at your materials you really need to ask yourself if this bureau is the right fit for you. I would hesitate to advise you to spend any money with a bureau before you know them really well. Ask other speakers for advice about specific bureaus. Be sure that you want to build a relationship with this bureau *and* that they are booking what you are offering. If they don't, then wait for them to come to you. Then you won't have to pay.

Getting the Business

. . . .

If a bureau has placed you on hold more than ten times without a booking, there could be two issues at hand: they don't know exactly how to position and sell you or your video is not competing in the marketplace. If it's the latter, then you will hear this from more than one bureau and know that your video (and possibly your speech) needs some work. If it's the former, then you might ask if you can spend 15 minutes on the phone with the sales team to help improve the closing ratio.

It's a very common issue for bureaus not to "get" what a speaker does. After all, they may have 20,000 speakers in their database. How can they possibly know every one? Make sure your marketing materials are doing their job and use the Positioning Page in Coaching Exercise 12 to provide the bureau with a clear understanding of how to sell you.

2.0 GETTING THE BUSINESS

After reviewing speakers' marketing materials (about ten per week for the past ten years), I suspect that your marketing materials will need work before approaching the bureau. They have to speak to the outcome of your work or else they will not get you booked. That said, a really good video can override a poor website.

The best way for a bureau rep to understand your work is to see you live. Without that, they may not "get" you. And if they are really smart, they are asking you what you can offer outside of speeches and will get a commission on the added value stuff. Not sure how many think creatively (beyond the speech), but when you get someone who does, build the relationship, cause they're a keeper.

Not sure how many bureau reps think creatively (beyond the speech), but when you get someone who does, build the relationship, cause they're a keeper.

Coaching Exercise 12: POSITIONING PAGE

It's a very common issue for bureaus not to understand what a speaker does. Make sure your marketing materials are doing their job and use this exercise to provide the bureau with a clear understanding of how to sell you.

The first column represents the speakers' bureaus' questions and requirements. The second column provides the bureau with the answers so they will "get" you and, in turn, be able to sell you.

Look at the Sam Seaborn example as a template.

Then, fill in the Positioning Page according to your business. This form may be used for in-house purposes, as well as for bureaus. Notice how the language in the sample is kept to a minimum — it's sparse and gives them just what they need. If you turn this form into three or four pages, you will lose the interest of bureau agents.

Sample Bureau Positioning Page: Sam Seaborn

When should I submit Sam for a program?	When the client is seeking a high energy speaker on the topic of motivation or peak performance. When a client wants to breathe some life into their organization.
Best Audience:	Sam works extremely well with sales teams.
What is Sam best known for?	Sam's book "The Seaborn System: Six Keys to Achieving Everything You Want" is a national bestseller.
What topics should Sam be listed under in our database?	Motivation, inspiration, sales, peak performance, sports/athletes.
What is most unique about Sam?	Sam's system was developed while he trained to compete in his first Iron Man triathlon. What made it more unique was that Sam was also recovering from a nearly fatal heart attack at age 35.
What parallels does Sam draw for a business audience, i.e., how does it relate to them?	Prior to his heart attack Sam was #1 in sales at ABC company. He was, like so many people in the audience, focused on the wrong goals.

When does Sam shine the brightest?	Sam is best at opening an event with extremely high energy that will last throughout the entire meeting.
When would Sam not be the best fit?	Sam does not fit during an after dinner (with alcohol) program.
What are the ROI results of Sam's presentations? What do clients comment about most?	Once employees apply The Seaborn System, they will improve their performance by up to 40% and they will lead balanced and more productive, happier lives.
What is the best sales/ closing strategy for booking Sam?	Sam's video consistently works to close business, but a phone call with Sam and the client can speed the booking along more quickly. Once the client speaks with Sam — it's a done deal.
Who is Sam most similar to?	Although he is different from them, Sam often shares the platform with people like Mark Sanborn and Simon Baily.

Positioning Page: _____   ***Date:*** _____

When should I submit _____ (your name here) for a program?	
Best Audience:	
What is _____ best known for?	
What topics should _____ be listed under in our database? What is most unique about _____?	
What parallels does _____ draw for a business audience, i.e., how does it relate to them?	
When does _____ shine the brightest?	
When would _____ not be the best fit?	
What are the ROI results of _____'s presentations? What do clients comment about most?	

What is the best sales/closing strategy for booking _____?	
Who is _____ most similar to?	

You can also find all of these exercises in a separate and conveniently bound workbook: *Wealthy Speaker Workbook and Planning Guide.*

⚡ FLASHPOINT: Cary Mullen

I had an insatiable desire to be in this business. My dad, who is my biggest champion, tried to talk me out of entering the professional speaking arena. "Cary, you just left a highly competitive world as a professional athlete — why would you want to dive into another one?" he said. At a very core level, I had just decided that I would be successful and I needed to make it happen. That did not mean that it happened quickly or without having to work through obstacles. In truth, it has been a long, hard battle.

Likely my lowest point was after being in the business full-time for two years and having a planning meeting with my business coach. We were looking through my financial results and realized that I was more than $50,000 in the hole for the year. It was scary to see the writing on the wall.

It was a trying time and the stakes were high: I was recently married, had a newborn son, and no cash flow. I was the sole income earner in our family and had left a good paying job to become a speaker. I was making advancements and improvements in my craft, but financially, I was moving backwards. My wife was understandably nervous and was questioning if continuing in this industry was the right thing; regardless, she took the leap of faith and supported me. Still, I had a clear vision and a belief that I could get there. I had made the decision that it was going to happen, regardless of the financial evidence around me.

I had gone from being the best in the world in sports to not being able to make ends meet.

While I believed that I would be successful, I realized that I needed to re-evaluate my strategy if I was going to win. I really needed to focus on a routine or process for winning just as I had done in sports. Don't misunderstand — there are critical relationships and tools that are required to get the attention of those who can hire you ... a dynamic, connected and highly effective marketing team and a great demo video are essential. However, if you don't have an internal, consistent and on-going approach to your speaking business, it would be like changing sports every four years and wondering why you can't make the Olympic team. Consistent focus has been at the center of all of my success.

When things started to turn around, it was because of what I now formally call a Process for Success™. At the center of the process is Focus, where vision comes into play. The other elements include Preparation — challenging limiting beliefs and visualizing success; Execution — building a winning team around me, building bureau relationships, and delivering on stage; Assessment — constantly asking for feedback to get even better; and Rejuvenation — celebrating my successes and revitalizing myself.

Now I feel like I am finally winning again. I am reaching my milestones, including earning great money. I realize that a combination of planning for tomorrow and celebrating today is critical for flourishing in the speaking profession.

The story isn't over ... in fact, it feels like I have just started to find my stride and I know that it will only get better from here! In the hundreds of races in which I have competed around the world, I was thrilled to stand on the podium once or twice a season. Now I stand at the podium almost every week of the year ... and it pays a lot better too.

2.0 CARY MULLEN

One important consideration regarding the professional speaking industry is the "home away" factor or the "being paid to ride airplanes" factor. Consider that once you've arrived you might not want to stay.

What I mean by that is that if you are successful you are generally delivering 50-100 speeches a year. That typically means 100-200 days on the road. For this reason many people finally get "successful" in the speaking industry but decide they need to modify their business model.

Personally I found it too difficult to deliver 50 speeches a year with a wife and (now) three little kids at home. I realized I was only making money when I was away from my family and I felt that my business model was flawed. I had not found it highly profitable to sell books, conduct training, handle consulting, or drive memberships. It meant I needed a major overhaul for me, and for my business. Even though my speaking business was successful, I decided to start to say "no" to some business in order to be with my family more.

But how? In the past I was a full-time speaker, and a part-time real estate developer. I shifted my priorities to be a full-time real estate developer and a selective professional speaker. We now live on the beach in Mexico for six months of the year, and I only speak in the spring, summer, and fall. My wife and kids have me home more, and we sell the dream of living on the beach. Speaking is a glorious and well-paid form of self-employment, but I decided to shift to being a business owner so I could be home at the supper table.

I shifted my main site from CaryMullen.com to VivoResorts.com. Now in speaking I get to help people succeed at higher levels, yet my development business is helping people that have already succeeded in finding their piece of paradise on the beach.

Consider your business model and how you want professional speaking to enhance it, and how it will impact your life in the best way.

BUILDING THE RELATIONSHIP

I've heard bureaus say that speakers are competing with them. It's true. A speaker or a speaker's staff is on the phone calling the same list of clients as the bureaus. That's why success in this industry, no matter which side you're on, comes down to relationships. If you, or your staff, call a client who says that they work with a bureau, tell them "Great, let us send you our information packet and we'd be happy to work through that bureau if you decide to book it." Inform the bureau of the conversation and your intentions. If you get booked, the bureau does the contract (keeps the relationship with the client) and everyone wins.

*I notice more and more that speakers who make working with them **easy** are the ones with whom meeting planners want to work. If the speaker considers the customers' desired outcome, then we've hit the jackpot! — Kris Young, Martin Bastion Productions/ Speakers Bureau*

Working the Gig

Once you have booked an engagement, working closely with the client, without the bureau agent's involvement, is not a true partnership. Keep them in the loop at every stage of the preparation for an engagement. After the event, introduce the bureau agent to the decision makers you've met on-site and allow that relationship to unfold. The bureau may get opportunities for business they would not have received without your introduction.

Trust

Issues that involve trust will arise over the course of working with bureaus. It's bound to happen. A bureau should trust that you are, indeed, going to hand over any spin-off business, just as you have to trust that they will follow up the leads you give them. The best long-term relationships are relaxed and involve mutual trust. A good motto for both bureaus and speakers is "do the right thing, even if senting you properly, then have a discussion with them to clarify roles. Over time, the bureaus that you enjoy working with will be the ones who book you most.

Spin-Off

All business that results from a bureau engagement goes back to the bureau. Notice I said *all business* — not some or occasionally. Without this initial piece of business, you would not have the spin-off. This also goes for product sales. Many bureaus will ask for 10% or 20% commission. The best way to get spin-off is to be really good — we've already established this fact. And use your "Help Me" speech. When someone hands you a card, make notes on the back and hand it over to the bureau. E-mailing all of the contact information from the road is a good way to go. By handing that card over early, the bureau agent can get the chance to develop a relationship with the client. Sending them a check after the engagement is booked is not the best approach. After you finish speaking, you should always call the bureau agent and let him or her know how it went and what to expect in spin-off.

If you asked 100 bureau agents who their favorite speaker was, many of them would say Joe Calloway. Why? Not only does he track his spin-off voraciously, he'll make sure a bureau gets a spin-off even if ten years have passed. On top of that, Joe's ability to be memorable on the platform has the client asking for him ten years later!

POST-GIG PROBLEMS

If you have a recurring issue with clients about travel or AV expenses, try to address them up front. For instance, air travel that costs over $1,000 may be a big issue for clients. Let the bureau agent know what your travel is going to cost (roughly) at the time of the booking so that they can educate the client. The last thing you want is for your final contact with the client to be one that is negative. Any problems with an engagement should be faced head on with a phone call or e-mail to the bureau agent.

GETTING PAID

Most bureaus will mail your speaking fee to you within two weeks after the engagement. If you are not being paid reasonably quickly by bureaus, call them to find out why. They should have received full payment from the client before the event date. If not, then they are not staying on top of things. If you feel uncomfortable working with a bureau because of delayed payment, then don't. It's like any business — you choose who to work with and who not to work with.

For more specifics on bureau deposits, agreements or cancellations, see Chapter 7 at Agreements and Contracts.

 ## GETTING PAID

Recently one of my University members told me about a booking with a bureau where he hadn't been paid, and he knew that the bureau had received payment from the client. The bureau was in financial trouble and my client was about to sue them. I told him that before taking it to court, he should make an effort to have a candid conversation with the bureau owner about his intentions to sue, which he did.

During the conversation, the bureau owner confessed that they had been having a rough quarter and they set up a payment schedule that was satisfactory to my client. Relationships mean a lot in the speaking industry. And knowing that bureau the way I did, I knew they were not being deceitful on purpose. People get into trouble. The lesson here is always proceed with caution before getting in too deep with an agency that is holding on to your money for you. And ask others for references.

BOTTOM LINE ON BUREAUS

Bureaus are a great way to build your name recognition in the industry and create demand so that your fee goes up. Once you get to the top, don't forget who helped you get there. Keep the lines of communication open, stay in touch and operate in the spirit of partnership and you will have brilliant bureau relationships that last a long time!

 ## BOTTOM LINE

Don't expect that the bureaus will be the answer to your prayers. They rarely launch or build anyone's speaking business to a major degree. They are struggling themselves these days, so my advice remains — get the business yourself and if they come calling, then that's beautiful!

7

GROWING YOUR BUSINESS BEYOND GIGS

That's it for the three phases in the Wealthy Speaker Process: ready, aim, fire. By this point you should have a clear picture of your expertise and position in the marketplace, you should have a killer speech, your marketing materials should be in place and your demo video (or clips) should rock, your database should be growing, and, with great exposure in the media and great gigs with the perfect clients, speakers' bureaus should be signing you up any day now.

So is that it? Is there more? Look back to page xix — A Day in the Life of the Wealthy Speaker. Does your typical day look like Your Day Five Years from Now (Coaching Exercise 2)? Or will it in the near future? If you answer "yes," congratulations. You've accomplished a feat many people never do. If you answer "no," we need to discover why not. Perhaps you want to grow your business further. Perhaps your image of that perfect day has shifted and you want to adjust your business model.

The discussion that follows in this chapter will allow you to continue to grow your business.

Developing Product

Products can be used as a promotional tool or to lend credibility and be a concrete example of your expertise. They can form a small or big part of your business. The type of products you offer may vary with your area of expertise, but some of the typical products are discussed here.

BOOKS

If you walk around NSA long enough, you'll hear it said that you must write a book in order to establish expertise. I wasn't sure if I believed that in the early days, but now I do. When a speaker doesn't have a book, I ask "Why?" Believe me when I say that I know it's not easy to write a book. *The Wealthy Speaker* took me a full year to produce. If you are a speaker who has a message inside of you that is bursting to get out, then a book is probably in your future. Many people fall into speaking once their book is written, but there is nothing wrong with getting your speaking business off the ground before writing the book, especially if you are not crystal clear on your central message. Speaking for a period of time will help you get focused. If you have ideas for three books, wait until you get a lot of audiences under your belt before you decide which book to write. The audiences will help you realize which one is most viable. Once again, you'll need to pick a lane.

Self-Publish or Traditional Publisher?

Before you decide how to publish your book, get clear on the type of book you want. A souvenir book is a product that you sell at the back of the room when your audience simply wants to take a piece of you home with them. Many speakers say that souvenir books do not get read so the quality of the book might be less than an expert book. I think that if you're going to put your name on anything, it should be of high quality. The souvenir book may have limited appeal to a publisher. With today's technology, the cost of producing this sort of book yourself is reasonable.

Expert books help to establish serious credibility in the marketplace. They position you as the voice of authority on your topic. This sort of book is likely to appeal to a broader range of readers and so fits with the traditional publishing house model.

Joe Calloway had made a nice amount of money from souvenir (back of room) books, but when Wiley & Sons approached him to do a book, he saw the value of having a publisher to take him to the next level in his speaking career. Despite the fact that he would make very little money from the Wiley book, it was a great move for Joe and did indeed bump his fees and credibility. Now when people call to order his old books, he tells them they are no longer in print because, in his words, "They worked ten years ago, but they are not the types of books I want my name associated with today."

I think that if you're going to put your name on anything, it should be of high quality.

Now that you know the difference, take the quiz in Coaching Exercise 13 to see which route is perfect for you.

2.0 PUBLISHING BOOKS

I want to throw a third option into the mix that I would call "Hybrid" publishing. Like self-publishing, you are still in charge of the content and you pay for the services. The difference is that "hybrid publishers" have their own logos, may provide some promotion, but have selling channels to distribute books to bookstores.

Having done self-publishing and hybrid publishing myself, I believe they each have value. The key question comes down to your distribution goals. Do you want to see your book in bookstores, or will you sell it

> **WEBSITE REFERENCE TOOL**
>
> **www.speakerlauncher.com** ➡
> **Book Buyer LOGIN** *(red button)*
> **Check Out:** Seth Godin at
> www.sethgodin.com.

mostly back of room or on your website? If it's the latter, then you might head straight for self-publishing.

If you'd like to get boned up on publishing, Seth Godin has written some very interesting blog posts. Check him out at www.sethgodin.com.

Coaching Exercise 13: PUBLISHING QUIZ

Before you decide how to publish your book, get clear on the type of book you want. A souvenir book is a product that you sell at the back of the room when your audience simply wants to take a piece of you home with them. Expert books help to establish serious credibility in the marketplace and appeal to a broader range of readers. Take the quiz to see which route is perfect for you.

Keep three considerations in mind when deciding which way to publish your book: time; credibility; and profit. Complete the quizzes to determine which method will work for you.

Quiz One — Expert Book

_____ Do I want to be nationally recognized as a leading expert in my field?

_____ Do I want to sell my books all over the world?

_____ Do I want to have a shot at writing a bestseller?

_____ I do not care how long it takes to publish my book?

_____ I do not care how much money I make on my book?

_____ I do not care if I have to give up some of the creative control on my book?

Quiz Two — Souvenir Book

_____ Do I want my clients and prospects to see me as credible?

_____ Do I want to have something to sell at my speeches?

_____ My first priority is not getting my book in stores?

_____ Do I want to make a lot of money from my book?

_____ Do I want my book to be published quickly?

_____ Do I want 100% creative control over the process?

2.0 *Quiz 3 — Hybrid Book* _____

_____ Do I want to have creative control?

_____ Do I want to make a little money on my books?

_____ Do I want my book published reasonably quickly?

_____ Do I want my book to get into bookstores?

_____ Can I afford to put some money behind my book?

_____ Do I want my clients and prospects to see me as credible?

If you answered most of the questions in Quiz One with "yes," then finding a publisher is probably the way to go. If you answered mostly "yes" in Quiz Two, then you are probably better suited to self-publishing. And, of course, if Quiz 3 felt like the best fit, then you'd consider hybrid publishing. This one is the most expensive of all of the options. There is more prestige in going with a publisher, but the odds of a publisher picking up your book are relatively low. A bestselling book could be the difference between a $5,000 keynote fee and a $25,000 fee, but again, the odds are not stacked in your favor. Clients may see a big name publisher as more credible than self-publishing, but you have to weigh all of the pros and cons and look at your goals. Finding a literary agent and writing a book proposal can take eight to twelve months. You don't always need a lit agent to get a publisher. Remember: you still have to write the book!

You can also find all of these exercises in a separate and conveniently bound workbook: *Wealthy Speaker Workbook and Planning Guide*.

Tips from the Masters: *CATHERINE LEEK*, *Green Onion Publishing*

Producing a Book as Professional as You

Advances in technology have made publishing a book yourself within the realm of possibility. It can still cost a pretty penny, but it is not nearly as expensive as it was fifteen or twenty years ago. However, producing a professional book is not a typical hardware store do-it-yourself project. If you are going to spend time and effort writing a book in hopes of self-publishing, it is worth your time and money to employ the assistance of accomplished experts to produce a professional book that represents you and your ideas in the most authoritative manner possible. While there are many stages in producing a book, having an understanding of the process will help you discuss issues and determine expertise from a more knowledgeable position.

An experienced editor or book designer will be able to manage the entire project for you. He or she will be able to contact multiple suppliers, provide quotes from which you can choose, liaise with all the parties, and ensure all details are handled. An editor or book designer who has worked inside a publishing house or in different capacities in the industry would be your best resource. While a project manager can alleviate a lot of the burden, ensure that you have final approval on the key decisions. For the purposes of the discussion below, we'll assume you've hired either an editor or book designer to take care of the business of managing the production of your book.

INITIAL MEETINGS

Writing a book, no matter how objective the material seems, is a very personal undertaking, so be sure that you click with the people with whom you are dealing the most — the editor and book designer. Spend some time on this step and interview a few candidates.

- **Editor** — Discuss the editor's experience in your genre and whether he or she has been involved in self-publishing before. A good editor will also have some questions for you, such as identifying your audience and purpose. The editor will have the biggest impact — after you — on your text, so be sure you are in sync.

- **Book Designer** — Ensure the book designer can handle the whole typesetting job, including the preparation of files for the printer and design and preparation of covers. A good designer will provide some samples; experience in the genre is helpful too. You will work closely with the book designer on very subjective issues, so ensure you choose someone with whom you feel comfortable asking questions and expressing opinions.

- **Printers, Distributors, Marketers and Publicists** — You may not need to meet with the printer or distributor, but you will want to meet with marketing and publicity to ensure they "get you."

QUOTES

Get detailed quotes up front, but know that these can change if the scope of the work changes. The project manager will provide you with a full quote for approval and it should be broken down into the following categories: editing, formatting, and printing.

EDITING

- **Before Starting** — Ensure you and the editor are clear on the audience and tone. Just as you did for your speech, you need to identify your very specific market or niche. The book should represent your tone and style and a good editor will stay true to these points. On a more technical note, determine how you and the editor will review material (i.e., tracking changes electronically).

- **Three Stages** — There are three stages of editing: developmental (focuses on structure; audience); stylistic (attends to flow of text; use of language); and copy editing (technical editing of spelling, grammar, etc.). The last two stages may be combined, but if your manuscript requires a developmental edit a separate pass will be required. The hardest part of this process for you will be letting go of the material. At some point you must say I am done writing — or you'll never see a finished book.

- **Process** — The best approach is one where you work together with the editor to ensure that you are happy with the editorial changes. The editor reads the manuscript through and discusses the approach with you. He or she then edits according to the guidelines discussed and provides you with an edited manuscript to review. This version of the manuscript usually contains some queries. After you review the edited manuscript, the editor makes a final pass, incorporating your responses.

FORMATTING

- **Interior Design** — When the editor and designer work together, the best results will be achieved. The editor creates a list of elements to be designed and includes notes on their purpose (how they aid the reader and/or look of the book) and also selects representative pages so the typesetter can create a sample. The interior design of a book can be of great advantage — it can aid in readability and help present the structure of ideas.

- **First Proofs** — The editor provides the final files to the typesetter. The book designer will format the text and ensure each page meets design specifications. Two sets of proofs are produced; one is forwarded to you, the other to the editor.

PROOFING AND FORMATTING

- **First Proofs** — In reviewing first proofs, the editor ensures nothing has been omitted, the interior design has been applied correctly, and page breaks are appropriate. You will be asked to review the material to ensure all the content is correct and up to date. At this point, stylistic editorial changes are discouraged as they become expensive and threaten the schedule. The editor combines your changes with his or hers and returns the proofs for correction.

- **Second Proofs** — The formatter makes the corrections and produces a second set of proofs. These are usually supplied to the editor only at this stage. The editor ensures all corrections have been made. The editor and formatter will continue this process until all changes have been completed accurately.

PRINTING, DISTRIBUTION, MARKETING AND SALES

The project manager will oversee the printing process. The project manager may provide names of freelance marketers/publicists. If you want to sell into bookstores, a distribution company is necessary.

As you can see, obtaining the help of qualified specialists will provide you with a team you can depend upon to produce a book that is professional in appearance and substance and that will represent you and your ideas.

2.0 PUBLISHING TIPS (Catherine Leek)

Over the years, not much has changed in the publishing industry in terms of how a book is created.

The author still needs to write it, an editor still needs to edit it, and it is still enhanced by a professional design and layout. At the next phase, a proof is created and the author and editor need to check that all is correct and up to date. And the book still needs to reach the public.

So, while the process has not changed and the relationships are still very important, it is how we work with the process that has altered thanks to technology. The editor and author should still have a conversation, but the editing process will be done by sending files and using functions like Word's Track Changes. No longer do we get paper proofs (anyone ever heard of galleys) but rather a pdf file is sent from the formatter to the author and editor. And finally you may not produce a printed book at all, but opt for an ebook and sell it online. Even if you decide to have a printed book, you no longer need a warehouse, as you can choose Print on Demand and print only what you need for this month's gigs.

So the message is still the same, only the medium has changed.

Master Catherine Leek *is president of Green Onion Publishing, helping authors take their ideas from concept to finished product. She has edited and managed the production of many self-published books and has worked in the industry for nearly 30 years.*

 ## PRINTING

Print on Demand, or PoD, has taken the publishing industry digital. Imagine this scenario. You work with a PoD printer (say CreateSpace) and send them all of your print-ready files and a set-up fee. They set it up and have your book ready for sale. Someone goes to Amazon and orders a copy of your book. The order goes directly to CreateSpace who prints the book and ships it directly to the customer. No middlemen means that you get a larger percentage of the profits. Cool hey?

Be very cautious when getting into this scenario to ensure that your book does not state "ships within 2-3 weeks" on Amazon. This is a sales killer. Do your homework to choose the best solution.

AUDIO

Every speech that you give, every workshop you do, every teleclass you lead is an opportunity to develop a product. Many speakers purchase a recording device and record every presentation they give. Why? Because you never know when you are going to be brilliant or the audience is going to react perfectly. Knowing your audience and what forms of learning they will pay for is key. Before you rush out, record something, and pay for packaging, do you homework. Take a look at your audience. Are they book buyers? Are they MP3 purchasers? Do they buy software? Or iPhone apps? Or assessment tools? If your target audience is teachers and they are book people rather than CD people, know that when you go into the product development phase. I've seen many speakers get an idea and jump the gun to produce a product, only to find it still sitting in their garage three years later. Ease into your product slowly. When you go to speak at a convention, walk around the trade show and ask questions to determine which products are selling and which are not.

VIDEO/DVD

How many times have people come up to you at the end of your speech and said, "I wish so and so had heard this speech." Videotaping a presentation and selling it is a great way to serve your clients while making some cash. Some speakers are afraid of losing speaking engagements if they sell a video, but I don't believe that a video on the screen is nearly as powerful as your live performance. While legally your video should be used for individual purposes and not group broadcasts, you can make a note to that affect on the package. Video can range widely in pricing — from $20 to $500. If your videos end up becoming training products, then set the pricing accordingly and offer a licensing package. Licensing agreements can be drawn up in a number of ways so make sure you study up before moving forward.

PRODUCTION OF YOUR PRODUCT

Before you can produce your products, you need to think about some of the practical aspects — packaging, pricing, distribution, etc.

Packaging

When doing your research, also note the standards for packaging. Some industries expect very fancy packaging, while for others there is very little. In our industry, speakers are used to buying content. They care more about what a CD is saying, than the package it comes in. And now that we have so much digital product, we may only be required to develop a jpeg of a product cover and no packaging at all.

Pricing

Again, do your homework. What are the standard prices for the type of product you are selling? I'm all for placing a higher value on your product than the industry dictates, this is part of positioning, but if no one will buy it, then what is the point? You'll see more on this below in Bundling.

One thing to stress when marketing a product is that people are not paying for the plastic or paper packaging around your product.

They are paying for the years of time that you put into developing this knowledge — make sure they are aware of that fact.

Distribution

If you are speaking to good sized audiences, then you may want to consider shipping products ahead to the engagement and selling at the back of the room. Meeting planners are usually supportive of this action, unless a speaker from a previous year has done too much selling from the platform. When clients pay big bucks for a speaker, the last thing they want is for that speaker to spend 15 to 30 minutes of speech time flogging his or her products. I can't say I blame them. However, if the client wants to help make the message linger for a long period of time, having the audience members take home a piece of you can be a win for the client and for you.

There are many ways to sell products at your speeches. You might give a few audience members some of your products as prizes during your speech (rewards for participation, etc.). You may hold a business card draw at the end of your speech. Or you may display your product at the front with you or at the back of the room. You can try to weave your product into your presentations ("in Chapter 4 of my book, I talk about …"). If you provide order forms to each attendee with the handout, then they can have a chance to consider the product while you are speaking. The best case scenario when you have a book is to have the meeting MC announce that you will be doing an autograph session after the speech. That technique raises the level of your celebrity and the audience is excited to talk to you and have you sign their book. It's satisfying for you and it helps the meeting planner develop some post-gig hype. More ideally you want the client (or a sponsor) to have purchased a book for everyone ahead of time!

In my experience about 10-20% of the average audience will buy something from you. That being said, your ability to sell and the type of audience could change this up or down several points. Once you have established an average, you can ship the appropriate amount of product. Have a checklist for product sales to ensure that you remember everything you need, such as signage, calculator, order forms, pens, cash box, credit card machine, etc.

SELLING YOUR PRODUCT

Selling Back of Room

There are ways to sell "back of room" that will leave the audience and client happy. David Knox, a real estate expert, has sold over a million dollars worth of product at his half-day events. He has the full retail set-up, including temp employees in each city. His method of selling is clear — to provide tremendous value throughout the speech and then leave three to five minutes before the morning break for his advertisement. People are very clear that he is in advertisement mode and he explains each product and its value. He's not trying to pull the wool over anyone's eyes. And the value of his product is what drives his reorder business, so he is quality conscious. The real estate world is conditioned for this type of sale, but not every market would have the same level of acceptance for this style.

There is a speaker in the industry who is a huge bestselling author and very famous. Whenever a meeting planner says to me, "We had a bad experience with a speaker selling product from the stage last year," I know immediately who they are talking about. Regardless of the value that this particular speaker was creating for his audiences — all the clients remembered was that he flogged his products from the platform for 25% of the time that he was paid — extremely well — to speak. Think about it this way: if this speaker was paid $25,000 for a 60-minute keynote, he was receiving $415 per minute. He spent 15 minutes — or $6250 — serving himself, rather than his audience.

When selling product from the platform, find the method that best suits your style, your audience, and, most importantly, your client. When you lead with value, everyone wins.

When selling product from the platform, find the method that best suits your style, your audience, and, most importantly, your client. When you lead with value, everyone wins.

Website Sales

Of course, back of the room is just one way to sell your product. Selling on your website is another option. Getting set up with a shopping cart, gateway, and credit card provider is usually the part that takes some time, perhaps more for small business owners in Canada than in the U.S. In my experience, the easiest way to go about this task is to find a shopping cart system first and then use one of the gateways and credit card providers with whom they link. The shopping cart usually has many providers to choose from and you should do your homework. Don't get sucked into a long contract at high credit card percentages.

Nowadays you don't necessarily need a swipe terminal, you can punch in the credit card information into a virtual terminal on your computer screen when dealing with order forms. There are also some apps developed for iPhones and Androids that allow you a virtual terminal. If you are doing relatively small amounts of product sales, then keep it simple. Over time you can bump up to a more sophisticated system. Many people start by using PayPal on their shopping carts and then move up from there. There's no reason to jump through all the hoops the credit card company sets up until you have the volume to justify it.

There are industry people who are very knowledgeable on the subject of selling information products online. And there is a formula for success: have one website per product. That being said, get educated on the entire process *before* proceeding down the road. The first step would be to decide exactly what you want your website products to do for you. Do you want to be an information marketer or do you want to focus on building your speaking business?

I was talking to a speaker a few years ago and showing her everything I had going on my website and the products I sell. This speaker currently charges $12,500 for a keynote and is speaking about 50 times per year. She kept going on and on about how great I was doing and how she needed to be doing all of this stuff. Finally I said, "Are you crazy? If I was making $12,500 per speech, do you think I would be messing around selling $20 CDs?" No. I'd spend my time booking more speeches. Keep things in perspective.

Most speakers use their websites to support the product sales driven by their audiences. The majority of your product sales will take place right after the speech. If that is the case, then keep your product strategy straightforward. When you have a major product, like a book, then it might be worthwhile to look at a marketing strategy for that product and possibly setting up an exclusive website just for it. I keep my technology coach close just for decisions like this. Keep your goals in mind and keep it simple. The gurus make cashing in on the information marketing boom look easy, but more and more people are finding that it is a tough business to crack.

> *The gurus make cashing in on the information marketing boom look easy, but more and more people are finding that it is a tough business to crack.*

BUNDLING

McDonald's figured out early on that putting a Big Mac together with fries and a coke made perfect sense. Now you rarely buy a burger outside of a meal deal. So how can you package your products in the same way? How can you add value for your customers while at the same time raising your revenue per person? Bundling is a great option.

Here are some things for you to think about when bundling products.

- What is the best way to offer value to my clients in a package or system?

- What products can I develop that compliment each other (i.e., book, video, audio combo)?

- What can I offer of my time to increase the value of my products?

- How can I develop bundles that all have a theme (i.e., sales bundle, teambuilding bundle, etc.)?

- Is there someone that I can partner with on a product to add to my bundle?

- Is there a product that I can purchase to add to my bundle to increase its value (i.e., poster, promotional product, calendar, etc.)?

- What products could I produce that everyone else doesn't have (i.e., iPhone apps, interactive web learning products, online assessment tools)? If you want to get inspired, keep up on the new iPad apps that crop up daily. For instance, reading the O Magazine on my iPad (complete with video and very cool interaction) changed magazine reading for me forever.

Think about how you can develop products with a bigger strategy in mind in order to double or triple your back of room sales. Developing one product at a time without any connection back to the strategy will probably not serve you in the long run.

My goal with *The Wealthy Speaker* (and 2.0) was never to sell one book at a time. My package of the book, workbook, and audio are always the goal.

Selling Sidebar

If you are reading this book and didn't buy the package, you might think, "Hey, I should pick up a copy of the workbook and audio." And so, why don't I make that easy for you by offering you a coupon? Please use coupon code: COMBO5

How can you make upselling a part of your products? There are typically options within your Shopping Cart that allow you to upsell at checkout as well.

Hiring Staff Who are Winners

With a few exceptions, most of the Wealthy Speakers in the field (top 1%) have a great marketing person or team behind them. When Vince and I were still working together, people always asked him, "How do I find 'a Jane?'" Tony Alessandra had Holli Catchpole (who was my idol when I first started in the industry), Larry Winget had Vic Osteen and Amanda Gore had Somer McCormick. Today, there's a whole new crew of staff superstars. How these people came together in the first place probably took some luck or synchronicity, but you want to do your best to hedge your bets when finding that perfect marketing person.

The hiring process has five steps:

1. Are you ready to hire?
2. What should this person do for you?

3. How much should you pay?

4. Who is the right fit?

5. Where will you find them?

2.0 STAFFING

I'd like to add a 6th question to this list and that is, do they need to be in-house, or virtual?

ARE YOU READY TO HIRE?

One of the most common things I hear from professional speakers is that they are not interested in marketing themselves. They'd like to hire someone to do it for them. For those of you who have tried to hire and failed, you know that this is easier said than done. Hiring, in any industry, is a crap shoot. Here are a few questions to determine whether you are ready to hire a marketing person to help build your speaking business.

- Are you losing business because you don't have time (or desire) to fill your business pipeline or follow up leads?
- Have you worked the business yourself for at least a year and know how to get bookings? Can you train someone else to do this?
- Can you afford to pay a base salary plus commission? Most good marketing people will not work for straight commission.
- Can you afford to make a mistake in hiring or will a bad choice put your business in jeopardy?

If you can answer "yes" to most of these questions then you are ready to take the next step.

WHAT SHOULD THIS PERSON DO FOR YOU?

One of the biggest mistakes speakers make when hiring is not getting clear on their needs until *after* they have hired. You need to be clear on what tasks you want this person to perform for you. Do you want someone to do the $10/hour jobs for you or someone to do outbound marketing? Do you want someone to pick up your dry cleaning? Or are you looking for a combination? Use the list of tasks in Coaching Exercise 14 to determine what your assistant should do. The lists are broken down into categories: getting speaking engagements; administrative duties; and personal assistant. At the end of the exercise you will have the beginnings of a job description.

Coaching Exercise 14: DEVELOPING A JOB DESCRIPTION

One of the biggest mistakes speakers make when hiring is not getting clear on their needs until after they have hired. You need to be clear on what tasks you want this person to perform for you. Do you want someone to do the $10/hour jobs? Or someone to do outbound marketing? Do you want someone to pick up your dry cleaning? Or are you looking for a combination? Use the list of tasks to determine what your assistant should do. The lists are broken down into categories: getting speaking engagements; administrative duties; and personal assistant. At the end of the exercise you will have the basis for a job description.

Get Speaking Engagements	Administrative Duties	Personal Assistant
• Prospecting • Cold calling/telemarketing • Marketing to and working with bureaus • Developing or updating marketing materials • Proposal writing • Sending out marketing materials or e-mail • Proposals (designing, sending out) • Closing deals (overcoming objections, etc.) • Meeting with clients • Mass marketing — mailings or e-mails • Showcase events • Following up leads from gigs • New product development	• Booking travel • Generating invoices/ bookkeeping • Schedule management • Gig logistics • Product fulfillment (shipping) • Database management • Newsletter management • Web site management • Managing other business interests/ investments, etc.	• Picking up dry cleaning • Feeding the fish • Keeping you organized • Arranging for baby sitters • Arranging family trips, etc.

You can also find all of these exercises in a separate and conveniently bound workbook: *Wealthy Speaker Workbook and Planning Guide.*

FLASHPOINT: Holli Catchpole, President, SpeakersOffice, Inc.

In 1984, when I first started working for Tony Alessandra, I was young and did not know a lot about the speaking industry. I started with administrative tasks and over time I started taking on higher levels of responsibility and gradually moved into sales and marketing. When I first started selling, Tony and I sat in the same area and I would listen in on his sales calls and his pre-program calls. That information was hugely valuable and shortened my learning curve dramatically. He taught me to always understand the "why" behind everything and that mind-set forced me to ask the right questions. Over time we started to think very similarly.

When we would look at the P&L, he would ask me what costs I would cut or what I would do to help the company grow.

I strongly believe that a speaker will always be able to sell themselves better than anyone else can, but through this type of training you can find a sales person that is very effective. You have to allow your team members some autonomy. I was allowed to make decisions. If I did something that could have been handled differently, we would talk about it and I would learn from it. It took about three or four years but, eventually, I moved into managing the company.

Tony treated me like a partner in the business rather than a staff person. In discussing important decisions, Tony would say, "What would you do if this was your company?" We constantly studied our profit and loss reports. When we would look at the P&L, he would ask me what costs I would cut or what I would do to help the company grow.

If speakers want to establish a relationship with a staff person, first and foremost they have to be clear on what they want this person to do for them. Do they want someone running their company, do they want a dedicated sales person or do they want someone to help do the administrative work? The bottom line is that they must know how to sell themselves and run their company before they hire employees to do it for them.

HOW MUCH SHOULD I PAY AN ASSISTANT?

If your job description includes tasks from all three areas, then you'll want to consider offering a base salary (for the administrative and/or personal assistant work) plus commission for the sales and marketing work. You may get creative and offer an admin-only person a bonus when you meet quotas.

One combination that seems to be successful is the "business manager" role that encompasses all three areas and pays salary plus commission. You and your business manager will grow the business together along with both of your incomes.

Embracing the Wealthy Speaker mentality means that when you have a staff person on commission, the bigger their checks are each month, the happier you feel, and the more the bottom line is growing. Make sure that you cut a fair deal so that you feel great about your staff earning an above average living.

WHO IS THE RIGHT FIT?

Now that you have a job description, make a list of the qualities that the person doing this job would possess. Then make a list of the values the person, with whom you'd work best, would possess. You'll notice that the people with whom you surround yourself often have similar values to your own.

It's important that you get very clear on the traits that your marketing person or staff will possess. Everyone interviews well, so you really need to spend some time with this person under unusual circumstances to see if they are who you think they are. A sample list that will help you get your list started appears a little later in this section.

Now That's a Job Interview!

I promised Vince Poscente that I would come to Dallas for an interview. I didn't really want to leave Vancouver, but I kept my promise and arrived on what seemed like the hottest day of the year. I went to see Vince speak at a local Meeting Professionals International event at South Fork Ranch (welcome to Dallas) and he did a good job. People seemed to really like him and the industry people in Dallas seemed very hospitable. I even gathered a few leads despite the fact that I hadn't accepted the job. From there my interview went a little like the movie *Sideways*. The fun began. Michelle, Vince's girlfriend who owned a speakers' bureau, accepted me immediately as a part of her family and they invited me to join them at a West Texas family reunion. We had one heck of a time. The following day we went tubing down the Guadalupe River and the next day we went to Mexico to drink margaritas. During the entire five days — I know you're asking "who has a five-day job interview?" — I had so much fun that the enormity of the move and leaving a high paying job to start over with a speaker who could barely afford me, wasn't on my mind. What I could see was that I would have fun with these people, learn a lot from the speakers' bureau, and there was a lot of potential for growth. I decided I had nothing to lose so I agreed and it has paid off incredibly.

Now I'm not telling you to ask your prospective marketing person to go tubing down a river with you. Seriously, no one wants to see their new boss in a Speedo! But allow the relationship some time to simmer. Make sure that you are compatible. Date them first. Allow them to show you their values over time rather than their good behavior during an interview. This is not something that you want to rush.

That being said, you are selling them on this position. Make sure that they can see the potential — that they will learn and enjoy working for you.

Possible Traits of Your Marketing Person

Here are ten ideas to get you started on your list. You'll have to be honest about your style and behaviors too.

1. **Honest** — Do your homework and have your prospective employees checked out. I know several speakers who have hired people who have stolen from them.

2. **Loyal** — You want someone who is in this for the long haul, a partner.

3. **Detail Oriented** — Just ask Vince about the time I sent him to Springfield, MO, instead of Springfield, IL — our motto

"details schmeetails" had to change quickly and I was forced to become a detail person.

4. **Sales Skills** — Anyone with a lot of sales training could be a fit.

5. **Relationship Builder** — In person and by phone they need to be able to build long-term relationships.

6. **"Gets" What You Do** — They understand the speaking business or at least have potential to understand. You want someone who is sharp.

7. **Able to Persevere** — The ups and downs of the industry will affect their income. Someone with support (and benefits) from a partner would be great.

8. **Risk Taker** — Someone who is safety oriented might not bode well with the ups and downs of commissions.

9. **Fun and Enthusiastic.**

10. **Able to See Opportunity Everywhere.**

If you are checking behavioral styles, like DISC, you might go for someone with a Driver and Interpersonal combination.

⚡ FLASHPOINT: Karen Harris, CMI Speaker Management

To build a strong and loyal relationship with your staff person or a management company and one that helps you generate more revenue for your business, regular communication from the road is crucial. We love to hear from our speakers live because we'll hear the excitement from the success of the event in their voice. This keeps us enthusiastic and passionate about the work that we do to support our speakers. We also ask for specific information via e-mail because it's very easy for a speaker to forget to tell us something in the excitement of the phone call.

Here are the most critical things we want to know and why we want to know them:

- Thank us for all we did to get you out the door. Acquiring information for some events goes smoothly — other times it does not! We need to hear that you appreciate everything we did to help you perform at this event.

- Was it a home run? Why or why not? We use the home run information when we're speaking to the next customer/bureau agent — "Carey just spoke for XYZ and hit a home run because ..."

- Were there any logistical hiccups with AV, flights, hotel? We constantly want to improve the little things that go wrong on the road so our speakers are free of hassle. This means they'll perform even better for the customer.

- How did back of room sales go? Or do you think they'd be interested in a product for each attendee now? Often a customer needs to experience a speaker before they will bring their products into their organization — we always attempt to do a post-event sale based on feedback from our speakers.

- Are there any leads for future events? We want to ensure that we or the bureau agent contact that prospect ASAP — it's important to contact them while the excitement of our speaker's presentation is fresh in their minds.

Communicating with your staff person/management company from the road helps them to feel involved and recognizes their contribution to the growth of your business. Remember, if they weren't doing these things, you'd have to do them!

WHERE DO I FIND THEM?

Now that you have a vision of your assistant in mind, here are some places to look for them:

- **Your Inner Circle** — Put out a notice for the type of person you seek to everyone you know in your business and personal life. If you attend a church, ask around there.

- **Your Audience** — Often someone who comes to talk to you after a presentation might be a candidate. You might even mention it from the platform, if you can turn it into a relevant story.

- **Speaker Management Companies** — It's getting more and more common for one person to manage several speakers. Ask around at your NSA or CAPS chapter to see who is in your area. The biggest problem these companies face is they cannot take all the speakers that come to them, so it's hard to get your foot in the door.

- **Advertising** — Locally or on a Monster.com-type website will probably get you a fair response. Make sure you mention that you are a professional speaker because people are intrigued by our industry. You'll have to weed through a stack of applicants, but it could find you that perfect person.

- **Staffing Agencies** — If you are prepared to pay the fees, then this is a great way to have someone else screen candidates for you.

2.0 HIRING STAFF

Do they need to be in-house or virtual?

Virtual assistants (VA) are popping up every day online and there are many who specialize in coaches and professional speakers. VAs are people who work from their home offices, sometimes from hundreds or thousands of miles away. They work with you using technology, such as Skype, Basecamp, and "the cloud" to do the jobs that you need done.

Nowadays it's become very common to have an entire team of VAs working with you.

Nowadays it's become very common to have an entire team of VAs working with you. That's what I do and it's such a relief not to have to find one person with all of the skills. As I've mentioned, my VA team has one leader and about six individuals who serve me in the areas of shopping cart, blog, website, graphics, audio/video, PR, social media, and editing. I love having one main contact and one person to pay at the end of the month. I know I pay more than the average VA charges, but it's worth it to remove the "hassle factor." People problems can often eat away at our time, so by reducing the number of people we manage directly, we reduce the "hassle factor."

Keep in mind the principle "hire slow, fire fast." Take your time. Be prepared to spend a lot of time training this person. This is why it's so important for you to know how to book speaking business. Do not bring them in, leave them alone and expect them to start booking business for you. That, most likely, won't happen. Have them come out to several of your speeches, read your books, watch your videos. Let them listen to you and role play with you prior to picking up the phone. Have a training agenda.

Hiring is like a marriage and the stats might even be similar (50%+ failure rate). So take your time, visualize the perfect person coming into your business and give them the training and tools to be successful.

> **WEBSITE REFERENCE TOOL**
>
> www.speakerlauncher.com ➡
> **Book Buyer LOGIN** *(red button)*
>
> Check out two of the people I admire most in this business: Holli Catchpole and Karen Harris. And my VA team, Biz Ease Support.

Speaking Agreements and Contracts

Your agreements should be thorough without being a pain in the butt for the meeting planner. If they have to bring in their legal team to review the agreement, then you are probably too intense. You want your agreement to stick, you want your clients to understand all of the money details and what happens if they cancel, but, at the same time, you don't want to scare them off.

In my 20 years, I have yet to hear of a speaker suing a client over a breach of contract. You should do your best to work things out to the client's (and your) satisfaction if they postpone or cancel.

> *Note to New Speakers*: Skim this section and come back to it later when needed. Your agreements can be fairly basic in the beginning and you will not need to worry about bureaus just yet. Much of this information — if you feel you need to have it all in place up front — will overwhelm you. *Don't let it!* You can ignore much of this and refer to it later.

COMPONENTS OF AN AGREEMENT

So what needs to go into a contract? Use the checklist below to ensure you include all the pertinent details. A copy of this list can be found in Coaching Exercise 15, along with a sample agreement. Refer back to these explanations as required.

- Your Name.

- Date of the Agreement.

- Client's Company or Group Name.

- Client's Contact Information — There may be one contact who signs the agreement (primary contact) and another contact on-site at the meeting (on-site contact). Allow the client space to give you both. Be sure to get cell and pager numbers if they have them.

- Event Date — You would be surprised how often dates can get mixed up. Putting the date in a specific format — Saturday, November 17, 2015 — can help ensure that there are no mistakes made with the date or day of the week.

- Speech Start Time and Finish Time — Be specific. When you leave these things blank or TBA (to be announced), you leave room for misunderstandings and when you get busy, this could become a problem.

- Other Time Requirements — If the client would like you to stay for lunch with the audience or participate in an awards ceremony or an autograph session, put it in writing. For celebrity speakers this becomes especially important. Every minute of your time with the client or audience should be put in the agreement.

- Title of Presentation — Putting this in writing may help you down the road if the client is ever questioning the content of your presentation. Make sure that they know what presentation they are buying.

- Speaking Fee — Place the agreed upon fee here as well as your deposit/payment policy. Most speakers ask for 50% down to hold or reserve the date for the client. The remaining 50% is due on the engagement date. You may send two invoices —

a deposit invoice and a balance invoice due on the engagement date. You will need to schedule a reminder notice for ten days before the event. Your invoices and/or your agreements should include to whom the check is made payable (company or speaker name), address to send check, and Tax I.D. Number. Putting the Tax I.D. upfront will save a step later.

- Cancellation Policy — This policy is in place to protect you if the client cancels at the last minute and it also protects the client if you cannot make the engagement. This is your policy, so it's up to you what you ask for, but I'll give you my ideal. The deposit of 50% is non-refundable unless you (the speaker) cancel. If the client cancels the presentation within 45 days of the event without rescheduling, then the balance is also non-refundable. You probably won't be able to book another speech to replace this lost income and you may have given up opportunities for paid engagements on this date. Here is some sample language:

  A non-refundable deposit of $000 is due by 00/00/00 to secure the reservation. If client cancels 45 days or less (without immediately rescheduling) before the engagement, the entire fee will be due. Although John Doe Speaker has never missed an engagement, in case of cancellation due to emergency, client will be reimbursed in full.

- Venue — Name, address, phone, and fax numbers. Your office may need to fax you something at the 11th hour. Always have fax numbers for venue and hotels in your file.

- Introducer's Name — This may go into the pre-gig questionnaire instead of the agreement. Either way you should gather this information.

- Audio/Video Taping Release — You may allow the client to audio- or videotape your speech, but be sure to ask for a high level copy of the master. Their copy of the videoe should be used for internal purposes only and not for resale. Putting this in the contract might spur them to arrange for filming when they hadn't thought of it, which is good for you. You should try to film everything.

- Air Travel — Traditionally, a speaker will book his or her own travel and bill the client for it after the engagement. If you are a busy speaker, then you probably need some flexibility in your airline ticketing. Therefore you might state in the agreement that you require a flexible (fully refundable) ticket. Some airlines do offer a choice of ticket type so that you can make changes without a hassle. You should tell the client in advance what the cost of the ticket will be so there are no surprises. Having a "no surprises" policy will avoid difficult situations after the final invoice goes out. The client really needs to know what to budget. Busy speakers often have enough points to upgrade to first or business class. Asking the client to pay for business class is your preroga- tive, but may be seen as arrogant if your speaking fee is the same price as the flight. My advice is to upgrade for as long as possible and avoid charging the client for first class tickets. For more on this see Setting and Raising Fees in Phase I: Ready. Again, a travel-included fee avoids all of this haggling.

- Hotel Address, Phone, and Fax Numbers (if different from speaking venue) — Typically, the client books the hotel room for the speaker and puts it and meals on their master account. The speaker pays for their own incidentals, such as movies, phone calls, etc. Therefore the agreement should spell that out. The agreement should always be clear about who is responsible for making the arrangements.

- Ground Transportation — A busy speaker will often have the client arrange for transportation in the arrival city. However, if the client requests that you make your own arrangements, then this is a point that is not worth fighting over. The greater your reputation, the more you will be treated like the "A" class player and cars will meet you at the airport. You can't force yourself onto the "A" class, it needs to happen organically.

- AV Requirements — An agreement should spell out every- thing that the client will need to budget for and AV could end up costing a few bucks. Spell out your AV requirements up front on the agreement, rather than have them find out later that you need a projector, etc. If you are the only speaker at the event, a projection unit could tack an additional $500–$1000 onto the venue bill so the client needs to know about this up front. You should also ask for the AV company's name either on the agreement or in your pre-gig questionnaire. The idea behind questions like this is — *no surprises*. When you are showing up to speak to 500 people and they intend to use a poor sound system and no professional AV, then you can try to negotiate a better situation for yourself. Sometimes it's the speaker's job to educate the client on how to get the best outcome.

- Handouts/Support Materials — Spell out in the agreement if you are going to provide handouts and if you want the client to arrange for photocopying, etc. If you have agreed to provide ten books as part of the agreement, this detail should go on the agreement as well.

Coaching Exercise 15: **AGREEMENT AND CONTRACT CHECKLIST**

Your agreements should be thorough without being a pain in the butt for the meeting planner. You want your agreement to stick, you want your clients to understand all of the money details and what happens if they cancel, but, at the same time, you don't want to scare them off.

Below is a list of items that should be included in every agreement and contract. Please refer to the text for more information. A sample agreement is on the next page.

- ☐ Your Name
- ☐ Date of the Agreement
- ☐ Client's Company or Group Name
- ☐ Client's Contact Information
- ☐ Event Date
- ☐ Speech Start Time and Finish Time
- ☐ Other Time Requirements
- ☐ Title of Presentation
- ☐ Speaking Fee
- ☐ Cancellation Policy
- ☐ Venue Address, Phone, Fax
- ☐ Introducer's Name
- ☐ Audio/Video Taping Release
- ☐ Air Travel
- ☐ Hotel Address, Phone and Fax Numbers (if different from speaking venue)
- ☐ Ground Transportation
- ☐ AV Requirements
- ☐ Handouts/Support Materials

Sample Agreement _____

logo

Speaker Agreement — Jon Duncan

CLIENT INFORMATION

Contact Person: Fontana James

Title: VP of Sales

Organization: ITMB Staffing

Address: 1444 Garland Rd., Dallas, TX 75226

Phone: 214-555-5552 **Fax:** 214-555-5551 **E-mail:** fontanaj@ITMB.com

Title of Presentation/Workshop: Secrets Of The Staffing Wizards

Date of Presentation/Workshop: Tuesday, January 21, 2015

Time of Presentation/Workshop: 1:00 P.M.—2:30 P.M. (90-Minute Program)

Location of Presentation/Workshop: Hotel St. George, Roosevelt Room

555 Hotel Lane, Dallas, TX 75666

The client agrees to pay the following fees and expenses:

The fee for this presentation/workshop is: $7,000

A non-refundable 50% deposit of $3,500 is due by 31/12/14 to secure the engagement date. If client cancels 45 days or less (without immediately rescheduling) the entire fee will be due as complete settlement. Should the speaker miss the engagement due to illness or emergency and a suitable replacement cannot be found, client will be reimbursed in full.

Deposit payable to: Duncan Consulting (Tax ID# 04-933333)

Address: 555 Wysteria Lane, Austin, TX 76229

The balance of **$3,500** to be handed to the speaker on engagement day.

Travel Expenses: Expenses include full coach airfare, meals, ground transportation and lodging. These expenses will be invoiced after the program. Jon Duncan will use his best efforts to keep travel expenses to a minimum.

Support Materials: Mr. Duncan's products, including books and tapes, may be made available for participants to purchase after his program(s), unless specified otherwise.

AV Requirements/Audio-Video Release: Wireless microphone, 6 foot table at back of room. Videotaping of Mr. Duncan's presentation is acceptable for internal use only. In return, we request a high quality master copy of the presentation.

Our signatures on this agreement indicate full compliance with the requests and the promises above, and complete understanding of the services to be provided.

_____

Client   Date

_____

Speaker   Date

You can also find all of these exercises in a separate and conveniently bound workbook: *Wealthy Speaker Workbook and Planning Guide.*

2.0 AGREEMENTS

Nowadays there are people who are entirely electronic. I love that because it saves trees. If you are not mailing a book with your agreement, you might want to consider making your PDF of the agreement "signature" friendly. That allows the client to sign it electronically and send it to you via e-mail.

And of course, money is also flowing more electronically now as well. The client may opt to send you an Internet Bank Transfer or PayPal. Make sure you know how much each payment method will cost you and if it's too high, opt for the old fashioned "check please."

VERBAL AGREEMENTS

Until you have a signed agreement as well as a deposit check, your agreement is simply a hold and should be treated as such. If another client comes sniffing around that date, then call the client and let them know that their date is not locked in until the paperwork is signed and the deposit is received. If the client is slow in getting the paperwork back to you, it is often a sign of lack of commitment. Do not turn down other engagements or stop taking holds for that date until you have the money in the bank! This is a lesson that I learned the hard way in my early days.

BUREAU AGREEMENTS

Speakers' bureaus will often fax you a firm offer prior to getting an agreement to you. If the client has signed the firm offer, then it should be as good as a contract. You should receive a formal agreement asking for your signature first and then a fully executed agreement (where all parties — most importantly the client — has signed) later. If you are not sure if the client has signed the contract yet, then continue to treat the date as a hold. You will learn early in your work with bureaus that some agents tend to jump the gun and tell you they have a deal before the client has signed the agreement. Believe it when you see it.

All of the same information listed in Coaching Exercise 15 should be on the bureau agreement. Read the fine print on the back of the agreement to make sure you are happy with it and, if not, scratch it off the agreement and initial it. You should let the bureau agent know ahead of time what you are not comfortable with and, hopefully, your relationship is strong enough to withstand the odd disagreement.

An example might be the bureau requesting that you not put any contact information on your PowerPoint presentation (your website URL). I would not agree to this because I believe the audience has every right to contact you directly after the engagement. Your relationship with the bureau should be based on trust and, therefore, they should know you will hand over any speaking business that results from that engagement.

BUREAU CANCELLATIONS

Make sure that you read the fine print about what happens in the event of a client cancellation. If it's last minute (usually within 30 days) then you are due some money. If the client wishes to reschedule, then you might agree to do so without penalty. It's typically better to come to an agreement about rescheduling than to try to collect cancellation monies.

BUREAU DEPOSITS

You most likely will not receive a deposit on bureau engagements. The bureau should be holding the deposit money in trust for you. This way, if either you or the client cancels, they can protect the other. You should receive your speaking payment within 14 days of your engagement. Some bureaus pay even sooner than that. Note the payment date on the agreement. If your payment is late, then call the bureau. They are holding your money and there is no reason why it should not be disbursed to you in a timely manner. See Chapter 6, Speakers' Bureaus and Event Planning Companies.

2.0 OVERSEAS ENGAGEMENTS

When working with organizations overseas, the agreement should be adjusted. You will want to get 100% of your fees and travel up front. If the money doesn't come through, then you do not get on the plane.

You may also request first class flights since you want to arrive at your destination feeling rested. And don't agree to speak the minute you arrive; give yourself a day to recover.

Your fees should double or possibly triple since it's going to take you a day to travel to and from the event city, possibly more. Make sure you are factoring in your time. International work sounds sexy and looks good on your bio, but is often draining. Check it out a few times and then decide how much overseas work is perfect for you in one year.

The High-Tech Speaker on the Road

I can't stress enough to beginning speakers that keeping your business simple in the early days is imperative. You can add bells and whistles with technology as you go. The majority of your income in the first few years should be spent on the speech and marketing.

Here are a few tools of the trade for the ultimate high-tech speaker.

1. Cell Phone (BlackBerry/iPhone).

2. Digital/Video-Camera built in to phone or separate.

3. Laptop.

4. Portable Printer. Under 5 lbs. designed for travel.

5. Presentation Software. You can use PowerPoint, Mac's Keynote, Prezi, or something similar.

6. Wireless Remote for advancing slides.

7. Projector/Lavaliere Mic. Some speakers do carry their own, but the clients will always provide them so it's not necessary to have them.

8. Digital Recording Device to audio record every speech. You never know when you are going to say something brilliant and you'll want to record it!

9. Business Card Scanner or iPhone App (Google Goggles or Abbyy). This might come in handy if you are constantly sending leads to speakers' bureaus.

10. Virtual Terminal or Swipe Terminal for product sales back of room.

11. Mobile Internet Stick. A USB that's hassle free for locations without wireless.

A DAY IN THE LIFE OF A HIGH-TECH SPEAKER

A day in the life of the high-tech speaker might look like this.

Pack suitcase for trip. Refer to Road Prep Checklist.

Carry-on luggage contains everything required for presentation.

Drive to airport.

While waiting in airline lounge (because you are a triple platinum member), do last minute prep for upcoming event on laptop.

Board plane and finish prep work. Answer e-mail.

Arrive in destination city. Check voice mail messages and return calls in taxi (or limo). Respond to any urgent text messages or e-mail. You receive e-mail notices that two holds came in via eSpeakers from your favorite bureau while you were flying.

Check into hotel. Boot up wireless in room and wrap up any remaining work.

Arrive at meeting room for AV check and set up laptop, wireless remote, projector, microphone, and digital recording device. Pass handouts and order forms to meeting planner and set up back of room for product sales.

Before going on stage, you receive a text message from the president of the group you are about to speak to telling you the outcome of a shareholders vote. This alters your presentation somewhat, but you are prepared for it.

Your presentation goes smoothly and all the technology works. Even if the power went out, you would still be able to deliver a powerful program — don't lean on technology so much that you would be ruined if it all failed. (This is where a printed copy of your slides might come in handy).

You stand at the back of the room autographing books and collecting order forms and business card leads for one hour. All of your leads go into your high-tech Ziploc baggie and order forms go into the brown envelope for the accountant.

You note that two orders need to be shipped from the office because you sold out. You scan the two business cards and send an e-mail to your office to get them shipped today (once credit cards have run).

You return to the hotel room and download the photos that you asked the meeting planner's assistant to take for you. You build a web or social media page for the group, which takes about five to ten minutes because you have a template, and send the meeting planner the follow up e-mail, which is also a template, with a link to your website. By the time the attendees get back to their hotel rooms or offices, they have a message from you with photos of their event. They think you are a wizard and surf your website, sign up for your e-zine and buy more product!

You scan the business cards that you have collected and send them electronically to the bureau who booked this engagement, letting them know the outcome of the presentation and how much spin-off to expect.

Meanwhile you check your ten new e-mails and see that one of the holds from this morning has already turned into a firm booking. You check the details of the event on eSpeakers and notice that you now have three days in a row in San Diego. You send a text message to your spouse and ask if he or she can join you for this trip. You then go back into eSpeakers and place the two days after the engagement on hold for personal time. Your assistant gets a copy of the hold and now knows not to book anything on those days. Your spouse and assistant both have your schedule at their disposal at all times through eSpeakers.

You answer your e-mail and decide to hit the pool for two hours before your airport transfer arrives.

How does this sound so far? And speaking of high-tech speakers, Scott Klososky takes high-tech to a new level when he incorporates it on stage. His use of Join Speaker makes his gigs very exciting and engaging, which turns into rave reviews, which turns into many more gigs and makes him a feature flashpoint.

2.0 ⚡ FLASHPOINT: Scott Klososky

Like many speakers, in my early years I did not seek to be on the platform giving speeches for a living. I was a technology entrepreneur who loved building startups then selling them. Along the way, I was asked to give a number of talks for groups on the new technologies coming out at that time (mid-1990s). One day I mentioned to an employee that I should get paid for doing these talks, and he introduced me to a friend of his who worked for one of the large speakers' bureaus. That led me to delivering a handful of paid keynotes each year for the next eight years or so. I loved being able to help people in this way, and after selling another company, I decided I wanted to speak full time.

One of the first steps I took was to engage Jane as a coach, and the rest is history, as they say. She helped me apply her model for creating a vibrant speaking business, and I went from doing an average of five paid speeches a year to netting over $1.3 million last year. To be real honest, that was faster growth and to a much more advanced level than I would have imagined. Some of that had to do with Jane's sage advice, the rest of it had to do with the fact that I focused on technology trends as a topic, and that is a pretty good subject these days.

As a technology speaker, I not only have a hot topic to discuss, it is also forever changing. That is both a blessing and a curse because it forces me to constantly update and retool my content, but also means clients can bring me back over and over and I always have something new to say! The other blessing is that I get to use technology to help improve the presentation.

I strongly suggest that you learn how to use systems like Joinspeaker.com in order to allow your audience to send questions and comments to you while you are on stage. This is something I have been doing for three years now and it creates a considerably more intimate relationship with the audience, and also a much better set of questions for you to answer along the way. I also suggest learning how to use something other than PowerPoint to deliver your presentations. I use Keynote and people notice the difference because the animations and transitions are noticeably nicer looking. Audiences today are impressed when you can elegantly integrate technologies like these into you presentation in order to create a better experience for them.

One more thought ... Social technologies are all the rage at the moment. By the way, that does not mean only Facebook and Twitter. Social technology tools and concepts go way beyond those two applications. Speaking for a living today means learning how to manage your online reputation, learning to connect online with meeting planners, bureau sales people, audience members, and large corporate clients, and learning to get work done by leveraging crowd sourcing. These are the social concepts that will really make a difference in building your business going forward. Don't get lost in the chaos of "experts" touting LinkedIn and Facebook as the only tools that matter in Web 2.0. There are many other tools, and a handful of powerful concepts, that will help you stand out.

There is no reason for a speaker to have work piled so high after every trip that they cannot keep up. Keeping your business flowing smoothly while on the road is not only helpful — it's imperative. Get the tools that will assist you in doing it. Pick and choose the items from the list above that would work for you and leave the rest. Anyone who says "you absolutely *must* have this item" might not know how your business works.

A note about accessibility: I am not a believer that you should be tied to your business and to your e-mail and text messaging. You have to have some down time away from these items. Teach your staff and your clients to expect that you *will* answer e-mails, voice mails and text between the hours of 8 A.M and 4 P.M. each day, but you *will not* answer messages after 4 P.M. until the following business day. Or you may only answer e-mails after 4 P.M. or whatever works for you! This is your business and your life and you may run it however you see fit. All access all the time doesn't always work, so find out what is perfect for you and then train the people around you about what to expect.

Tips from the Masters: *JOE HEAPS AND DAVE REED, eSpeakers.com*

Technology You Must Have to Run a Sustainable Speaking Business

We don't believe in technology, at least, not for its own sake. Technology should be a means to an end — a long-term, profitable speaking business. If you've talked with other professional speakers about the technology they use in their business, you may have talked with "enthusiasts" who get excited about having the latest gadgets or services. Some of these leading-edge tools are useful; some are a waste of time and money (unless you enjoy them just because they're neat). You may also have talked with technophobes who do everything on paper and "have gotten by just fine going on 50 years."

We've been helping speakers with the business technology in their offices since 1999 and have found three core technologies that every successful speaker's business uses to run efficiently and to give a superior service experience to their customers. There are tools outside of these three that are useful and can help you build your business, but a sustainable speaking business needs *at least* these three to survive. If your current chest of business tools does *not* include each of these three core pieces, you'll either have trouble giving your customers a truly professional experience or you'll waste money doing it. Those are dollars you could be using for marketing and growth.

1. CONTACT MANAGEMENT SOFTWARE

Contact Management software is designed to store *people* and so it allows information about the people with whom you want to grow productive business relationships. You can store multiple phone numbers, e-mail addresses, notes about conversations, and key pieces of information on each client or prospect.

Contact managers are crucial during the sales cycle. At any point in time you'll have several potential customers at some stage in your sales pipeline. Your contact manager will help you move them through the pipeline until they become a sale or don't. It does this by storing what your last contact with each prospect was, what and when your next follow-up contact should be and then giving you some sort of reminder when it's time to make a call or write an e-mail. If they don't book you this year, you'll need a reminder to contact them about their meeting next year.

Key features to look for in a contact manager:

- full and customizable compliment of details for each contact record: multiple phone numbers, e-mail addresses, and addresses;
- unlimited "notes" area for each contact record where you'll keep notes during phone calls or copy (or attach) e-mail;
- your smartphone needs to be able to synchronize with it so you have an up-to-date copy of your contacts wherever you are;
- if you have multiple folks in your office, it should be multi-user compatible so that each user can have simultaneous access to the contacts; and
- a "to-do" list that provides a pop-up or e-mail reminder when it's time to make a contact with one of your contacts.

Frequently seen in speaker's offices:

- ACT!,
- GoldMine, and
- Outlook.

WEBSITE REFERENCE TOOL

www.speakerlauncher.com ➡
Book Buyer LOGIN *(red button)*
Check Out: Act!, Goldmine, Outlook

Sales are a crucial part of a successful speaking business and sales are all about people. If you don't already have a contact manager that you're in love with, we recommend ACT!

2. EVENT MANAGEMENT SOFTWARE

Once your contact manager helps you close a sale, you have a new type of information to manage — an "event."

Event management software takes care of what many speakers refer to as "the calendar," but a good one does much more than just keep track of dates. A speaker's calendar is his or her inventory, just as books are for a bookstore. As such, it's a lot more complex than a normal "calendar" that you might find included with other software (like your contact manager). You've got to track not only sold dates, but also manage held dates, releases, travel days, and personal days not available for sale.

Event management software should keep this complex calendar, along with the myriad details that go with each booked date (like travel, audience composition, services and prices, pre-event phone call, etc.). Event management software should track what services you're selling to the client and for how much. It should track any product that you're selling at or to the event. It should track the boxes in which product is shipped. It should have a notes section that lets you make notes during phone conversations or paste in copies of e-mail that are related to the event (this is different than notes related to a contact).

Although events are very different animals than contacts, they are *related* to contacts and so your event manager should be able to talk to your contact manager. It should also synchronize with your smartphone so you can carry your event details with you easily.

Key features to look for in an event manager:

- full details about individual events (notes, travel plans, customer pricing, etc.);
- full support for a speaker's calendar: multiple holds on same day, booked events, personal "blackout" days;
- it should integrate with popular contact managers, allowing you to attach contacts to your events;
- it needs to synchronize with your phone so you have your calendar and event details wherever you go;
- if you have multiple users in your office, it should be multi-user compatible so that each user can have simultaneous access to the event details;
- if you have office staff that live in a different city or state, it should give them virtual office capabilities as if they were there in your office in person; and

- full suite of reports that help you track the progress of your business.

Frequently seen in speaker's offices:

- custom software applications based on a programming language like Access or FileMaker Pro (speakers hire a software developer to build and provide ongoing maintenance),
- EventProtm, and
- a combination of Outlook, Excel, Word (does not provide many of the key features).

The more effectively you can manage your clients and the information associated with their event, the better you can service them. Superior service turns into happy customers, which turns into repeat business. If you don't already have a good event manager, it's no surprise. We recommend using EventProtm from eSpeakers.

3. FINANCIAL MANAGEMENT SOFTWARE

Now that you have an effective contact manager to help you make sales, an effective event manager to help you manage your inventory and gig details, you need a way to keep track of all the money that's pouring in!

Good financial management software should keep track of your checking and/or savings accounts, your accounts receivable, and your accounts payable. Your finance software not only makes the job of dealing with money simpler (computer printed checks, automated reconciling with your bank, etc.), it gives you useful ways to track your budget and spotlights places you may be wasting dollars.

WEBSITE REFERENCE TOOL

www.speakerlauncher.com ➡
Book Buyer LOGIN *(red button)*
Check Out: eSpeakers

One big time saver is online checking account reconciling. Make sure your bank provides that service. Balancing the checkbook becomes a matter of pushing a button and having your software talk with the bank to find out which checks cleared and which haven't, and ensuring checks cleared for the proper amount. The few hours a month you might spend doing this yourself, or the dollars you'd spend having an accountant do it, can be spent on marketing and growing your business.

Some financial management packages make it easy to process credit cards. This is very useful, especially if you have products like tapes or books that you sell to clients independently of an event.

Key features to look for in financial management software:

- directly prints checks on your printer;
- can communicate with banks for checking account reconciliation;
- full suite of business reports;
- easy to use (some packages are feature-rich, but require an accounting degree to use properly);
- exports to popular tax preparation software (this can be a big time saver at tax season);
- generates invoices for customers; and
- if you have employees, your package should have payroll features.

Frequently seen in speaker's offices:

- Microsoft Money Small Business and
- QuickBooks.

Without good financial software, keeping track of what money is owed you and whom you owe can become a job in itself — which means less time growing your speaking business. We recommend QuickBooks if you don't already have a package with which you're happy.

Technology can be daunting when you first get started, but if you run your business out of a shoebox, you will have a hard time growing. We hope that these suggestions will help you develop a system that will bring your office to a new level of organization, flow, and customer service.

TECHNOLOGY TIPS (Joe Heaps and Dave Reed)

We believe that running a sustainable speaking business means being an early adopter of new technology tools. If you wait to see what other speakers are doing with it, you're going to get left in the dust. One of the new technologies that we think is absolutely essential for your office is cloud computing. You're probably already using cloud computing and may not even know it. In essence, cloud computing means having every piece of data you need to run your business and your life at your fingertips and ready for use. We recommend that your e-mail, contacts, accounting, calendar, and event management all be "in the cloud." Once in the cloud you can access them from your smartphone, desktop computer, laptop computer, or iPad on the fly.

Here are a few tools that we suggest using in your quest to be on the cloud and run a successful speaker business.

- Office Apps: Google Apps, Microsoft Office 365, ZoHo Docs
- Contacts: Google Apps, SalesForce, InfusionSoft
- Calendaring/Scheduling: eSpeakers, Google Apps, Office 365
- Accounting: Quickbooks online, Freshbooks
- Event Management: eSpeakers
- Data Storage: JungleDisk, Dropbox, Skydrive
- Online Media Kit/Profile: eSpeakers

Master Joe Heaps *is the VP of Business Development and Master Dave Reed is the Technical Director for eSpeakers. Both are experts on the use of technology in the speaking profession.*

WEBSITE REFERENCE TOOL

www.speakerlauncher.com ➡
Book Buyer LOGIN *(red button)*
For links to the above websites.

BEING A BETA TESTER HAS ITS BENEFITS

Several years ago Art Berg, a hugely successful speaker, approached Vince and I to do a beta test of his new online calendar tool for speakers called eSpeakers. We agreed and spent several years trying out programs for the designer Dave

Reed. I'd call Dave and say "I love this new feature Dave, but you know what would be really cool ..." and, sure enough, the next version of the program would have my suggestions. Art Berg died tragically a few years into the eSpeakers EventPro product launch, but his vision has gone on and, for busy speakers, there is nothing better to help manage all of the aspects of their events. And it's because I've had first hand experience in the development of this program that I know it's awesome.

MAKING TIME FOR YOUR BODY WHILE ON THE ROAD

A speaker named Jason Womack told me that when he travels (100 dates per year), instead of setting up his computer on the desk in the hotel room, he lays out his workout clothes. That way, rather than getting sucked into the computer (which we think will only be 15 minutes, but usually turns into two hours) he goes to the gym or for a run instead. These are the types of tips that road warriors need to know in order to thrive on the road.

Plan out your travel days just as if you were at home and make sure that you plan some healthy activities. Some speakers speed walk at airports, some take their own food on the road, while others do yoga in their room, or use the hotel swimming pool. Don't leave your health to chance while on the road or, before you know it, you'll be having a hard time squeezing into that airplane seat.

Being a Super Hero

The speaking industry is full of super-humans. There are people who are high achievers and accomplish much more in a day than us mere mortals. I remember a speaker friend once saying, "It's lonely at the top." At the time I didn't understand, but now I do. When the thousands of people in your audiences each year are looking to you for the answers, it does get lonely. They've put you up on a pedestal. Where do the motivational speakers go to get their motivation? How can they go home at night and admit "I don't have the answers" or "I'm struggling?" Well, it's not easy to do, but the bottom line is to *keep it real*. (Vince Poscente modeled "real" for you in his 2.0 update in Phase I: Ready).

You must speak honestly to the people in your corner — your friends, family, and colleagues. When you arrive at the next speakers' gathering, I challenge you to tell the truth when someone asks you how you are and not the glossed-over version. Slow down and concentrate on being a "human being" rather than a "human doing," If you feel pressure, it's because you've placed it on yourself. Fall off the stage every once in a while; that seems to work for keeping it real.

Recently I coached a speaker who told me with great bravado that he gives 326 speeches per year. He was actually proud of that number! I was not impressed — especially when it came out that 50% of those were freebies, meant to sell product. With a little more probing, it turned out that he actually gave 45 full-fee speeches at $2500 a pop. Now that's more accurate. This guy showed up with his "super-speaker" mask on, trying to impress me with this giant number. I hope that you don't ever do that — keep it real, please!

When I first finished coaching school, many years ago, and started building my coaching and consulting practice, business came to me relatively easily. Within about a year, my colleagues from school were still struggling, and I had a full client roster and had raised my fee three times. I had started with 12 years of knowledge under my belt, so I leaped to the front of the pack with very little effort. When I went back to Vancouver for my coaching class reunion, I strutted around like a peacock, so proud of myself and eager to share my success story. I would never have said, "Well, I'm actually having a hard time with…" I was too busy displaying perfection. I don't remember when it dawned on me that I was being a complete phony, but it did. I realized at that point that I had been full of crap for years. I wore a social mask that said, "All is well with me. I am a successful superstar."

Getting real took some practice. I took a writing class in preparation for this book. I wrote about moving to a new city, which I had just done for the eighth time in 15 years, and how this time I was going to get real and actually live! When I read the story to my parents, it was so honest and raw that we all cried. And from there forward, I had permission to stop being super-daughter, super-coach, super-friend and start being a real person with flaws and challenges just like everyone else.

It's ironic that an ordinary Jane like myself would have something to share with an industry full of over-achievers. But by this point in the book, I am sure you have benefited greatly from the mistakes and successes that I have had in this industry. I hope that before you go off half-cocked on your next marketing endeavor, you will ask yourself a few questions. Am I doing this because some industry expert told me to or because it fits with the goals of my business? I hope you have learned to get Ready, take Aim and then Fire.

When you go out into the world as a professional speaker, my wish for you is that you can show up to your audiences as an authentic human being (flaws and all) who has an incredibly important message to share. Your audiences will appreciate you being real — even if you do fall off the stage every once in a while!

Acknowledgments

• •

There have been so many people who have impacted my career — I'll apologize in advance for those that I've missed. I've attended conventions and workshops with the National Speakers Association and Canadian Association for Professional Speakers for nearly two decades. People like Thom Winninger, Rosita Perez, Barb Schwarz, Les Brown, Tom Stoyan, Gerry Coffee, Larry Winget, Lou Heckler, Art Berg, Marc LeBlanc, Peter Urs Bender, Doug Stevenson, and Warren Evans are just a few who've made an impact on my career.

My employers, right from the beginning, have been tremendous mentors and partners. Huge thanks go out to Betska K-Burr, Peter Legge, Vince Poscente, and Michelle Lemmons-Poscente. You are all incredible talents. I have been honored to know you, learn from you, and work with you.

My life coach, Rich Fettke, helped me design and deliver the business and life of my dreams.

My bureau colleagues have helped move many of my speakers and clients up the ladder. Thank you all, and especially to the team at ISB who taught me so much.

My coaching clients are too many to mention. You inspire me every day and I thank you for the great work that you do in this world.

My Master Partners on this project were outstanding: Victoria Labalme, Robin Creasman, Catherine Leek, Joe Heaps and Dave Reed, and Kris Young.

The contributors to this book were amazing with their honest and helpful stories and quotes. I thank Ryan Estis, Toni Newman, Rick Butts, Bob Parker, Greg Schinkel, Patricia Fripp, Vince Poscente, Amanda Gore, Peter Legge, Keith Harrell, Mike Pniewski, Mark Sanborn, Somer McCormick, Cheryl Cran, Gail Davis, Mark Levin,

Cary Mullen, Holli Catchpole, Karen Harris, Brian Palmer, Theresa Beenken, Martin Perelmuter, Art Berg, Thom Winninger, Scott Klososky, and André Shahrdar.

I would be remiss not to mention my friend Joe Calloway who so generously shares his story. I'm grateful to have spent so much time with one of the best business minds in our industry.

Thanks to David Chilton for giving me his blessing on my title, *The Wealthy Speaker*, back when I first went to print.

Catherine Leek — continues to be my extraordinary editor. Once again, you made the process amazingly simple. Heidy Lawrance and her design team, Beth and Kim — geniuses! Tim Handleman for an awesome original cover, Beth Crane for the 2.0 cover, and Steve Morris for his cartoons. Rick Butts was the brilliant one who came up with this book's title — thank you. Shelle Rose Charvet, my NLP coach, helped me tremendously with language on the book cover and back.

My business would be nothing without my VA team, led by Terry Green. They are the glue that holds it together on all sides of my business.

And, of course, my mom who is my biggest cheerleader and my dad who continues to cheer for me from up above. I could never have done this without your love and support along the way.

And the biggest change since the original *Wealthy Speaker* is that now I get to thank my husband of five years. John, you are my inspiration. Thank you!

53184028R00157

Made in the USA
Charleston, SC
05 March 2016